W·I·N·N·I·N·G
*D*OUBLES

Also by Scott Perlstein:
Essential Tennis

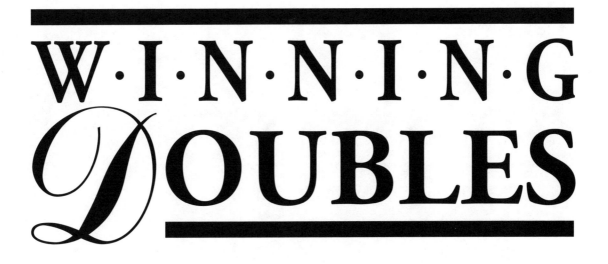

WINNING DOUBLES

SCOTT PERLSTEIN

Edited by Joanne McConnell

THE LYONS PRESS
GUILFORD, CONNECTICUT
AN IMPRINT OF THE GLOBE PEQUOT PRESS

The Lyons Press is an imprint of The Globe Pequot Press.

Interior design by Howard P. Johnson, Communigrafix, Inc.

Library of Congress Cataloging-in-Publication Data

Perlstein, Scott.
   Winning doubles : strategies, key concepts, and shot-by-shot
playbook for players at all levels / Scott Perlstein.
     p.   cm.
  ISBN 1-55821-330-9
  1. Tennis—Doubles. I. Title.
GV1002.8.P47 1995
796.342'28—dc20

                              94-48146
                                CIP

Manufactured in the United States of America
First edition/Fourth printing

DEDICATION

To my wife Karen, who lets me play at my computer to write these books. To Kevin Conway, Bruce Maxwell, and Mark Jee, my three long-term doubles partners. To Tim Gullikson, who lets me hang around the pros. And to my students and the game of tennis.

Pictured:

Kathleen Camarata
Chris Caputo
Linda Clark
Ray Ernst
Danny Ganoza
Brian Johnson
David Luther
Katherine Mankiewicz
Karen Woodell Perlstein
Maury Perlstein
Debra Vinci

Photos by Mark Perlstein

C O N T E N T S

· · · · · · · ·

FOREWORD BY RICHEY RENEBERG   ix

INTRODUCTION   1

1 THE ELEMENTS OF DOUBLES   4

2 THE PLAYERS   16

3 THE PARTNERSHIP   27

4 DOUBLES STRATEGY   36

5 THE PLAYBOOK   40

6 PLAYING YOUR BEST TENNIS   166

7 CORRECTING MISTAKES   179

AFTERWORD   185

APPENDIX A:
     USTA LEVELS OF THE GAME   187

APPENDIX B: SCORING   189

APPENDIX C:
     USTA CODE OF CONDUCT   190

· · · · · · · ·

*F*OREWORD

play doubles. I like doubles. I
like the interaction with a partner—that he can pick me up on some
days and I can help him on others. I like the quickness and pace that
doubles action brings, as well as the strategy and movement.

I won my first national title in doubles at age 11, and since then
I have always played doubles in my tournaments. Learning to play
doubles has made me a better player—especially in college, where I
could contribute to my team in both singles and doubles.

Since 1987 I have been playing both singles and doubles on the
men's ATP (Association of Tennis Professionals) tour. I have had good
success in singles, but it is in doubles that three achievements stand
out. First, in 1992, Jim Grabb and I won a Grand Slam title, the U.S.
Open. This was a particularly special win for us after losing the Wimbledon doubles championship just two months before in a close,
19–17 fifth set. It was also nice to win the Grand Slam in our own
country. Then, for 12 weeks in 1993, I held the number one doubles

ranking in the world on the ATP computer rankings. Although I didn't feel any different, as one of my friends pointed out, being number one in any endeavor is a fantastic achievement that few can ever claim. Finally, what I consider my biggest doubles achievement: In 1993 and 1994, I was fortunate enough to represent my country as a member of the Davis Cup doubles team.

I met Scott Perlstein through a mutual friend and have known him for over six years. I've been on the court with him and I've seen him work. His ability to explain the entire picture, then break it down into smaller, achievable increments, is as good as any coaching I've seen.

In *Winning Doubles*, Scott addresses the keys to being a good partner, learning to work together as a team, and improving as a team. Most important, he presents a clear playbook that, if followed, will help you understand the plays that you must create and follow to have the success your team desires.

—Richey Reneberg

W·I·N·N·I·N·G
DOUBLES

INTRODUCTION

Monday, July 6, 1992. The setting: the All England Club. The tournament: Wimbledon, the oldest and most prestigious tournament to tennis fans and players alike. The tournament was supposed to have ended the day before. But due to an incredibly long and exciting doubles final between the teams of John McEnroe and Michael Stich and Jim Grabb and Richey Reneberg, the tournament is not over. Not only has this match carried over from the day before, but the fans have been let in for free to witness the conclusion. This is the "deal of the century" for tennis fans, because Wimbledon tickets are the toughest Grand Slam tournament tickets to obtain.

The players had tried to end the match the night before, but neither team could gain the two-game lead required for the win. Finally, as night fell, the match had to be suspended. It was so dark that the players could barely see the ball, and the television commentators were afraid that the lights on the cameras would not provide enough illumination for the viewers to see anymore play. The score at this point was two sets apiece. Grabb and Reneberg had won the first and third sets 7–5 and 6–3. McEnroe and Stich had won the second and fourth sets, both in tiebreakers. At 13 all in the fifth set, the players met at the net, and tournament referee Andy Mills was called in.

McEnroe and Stich finally prevailed 19–17 in that fifth set on Monday—ending the longest doubles match in Wimbledon history. It took over 5 hours to complete, not to mention the extra day. Believe it or not, this famous match fell shy of the longest doubles match in pro tennis history, which was played in February 1968 in the men's doubles quarterfinals of the U.S. Indoor Championships at Salisbury, Maryland. Mark Cox and Bobby Wilson defeated Charlie Pasarell and Ron Homberg 26–24, 17–19, 30–28; a total of 144 games were played in 6 hours and 23 minutes.

Doubles is not always an all-day affair—the shortest match was played on July 13, 1914, in the men's final of the Kent Championships at Beckham, when Norman Brooks and Tony Wilding defeated Arthur Gore and Herbert Roper Barntt 6–2, 6–1 in just 16 minutes. This match was played before the teams were given the 20-second break between points and the 90-second changeover rest after the completion of each odd numbered game.

Whether you are a pro playing on the grass courts of Wimbledon or a young, less seasoned player playing on the Har-tru courts of Central Park, doubles is one of the best ways to have fun, spend time, and meet people.

Every year I attend the Newsweek Championships in Palm Springs. Before the format was changed in 1994, the crowd usually started to leave by 4:00 P.M., just when doubles would begin. By 6:00 P.M. the stadium would be nearly empty, which was great for my wife and me and our traveling companions the Rosenstocks, because we could move down to courtside to watch the rest of the matches. By 7:00 P.M. the stadium would look like an "MCI plan"—friends and family only! At this point, as sports announcer Al Michaels once said, "Instead of giving you the paid attendance, it would be easier just to tell you who is here."

We never leave until the last ball is struck, because the quality of hitting is unbelievably great. Being that close to the players, with so few fans around, we actually feel as if we are a part of the action. This is, in my estimation, the best part of the tournament—doubles. Why the fans leave and miss the doubles events is a mystery to me. Watching high-level doubles competition can be instructional, inspirational, and, as described before, exciting and dramatic.

I teach tennis six days a week, sometimes 10 hours a day. One of my prime motivators is my dedication to improvement. I must stay current and continually work to improve my game, which gives me a huge marketing advantage over so many other teaching pros. I take time off from my business and my students to attend at least three major pro tournaments a year, and it's the doubles events that I enjoy the most. I also continue to play tournaments with my partner of four years, Mark Jee. We both enjoy the competition and the camaraderie, and we have never had so much fun on the tennis court. The combination of watching highly competitive players and being one not only helps me stay up-to-date but also helps me maintain my enthusiasm for the sport. This enthusiasm spills over to my students.

Doubles requires teamwork and quick action, but many times four players walk onto the court and begin playing tennis without really knowing how doubles is supposed to be played. That's why I wrote this book. Its purpose is to help the reader (player) become a better doubles player. This book addresses all levels of the game. Whether you are just beginning or playing on the tour, you will advance your game to another level if you learn the lessons between these covers. I discuss the kinds of doubles played, positioning, movement strategy, and how to help yourself and each other be better doubles partners. I also discuss various problems that develop on the court between opponents and partners and how to handle these situations.

The most important element of this book is the picture playbook for doubles strategy. If you ever played football or basketball, you had a playbook to study to follow patterns that can develop during the game. I have set up 64 play scenarios that occur on the doubles court, showing both teams how to move and respond to each situation. For every scenario you will be taught the shot to hit, where to place that shot, and where you and your partner should position yourselves on the court for the return of your shot. There is also a set of pictures to help your team better understand the situation presented. I often compare these play scenarios to the loading of a floppy disk onto a computer. It takes a little time to load the program, and it also takes time to learn to use the computer program. But once loaded, you can just turn the computer on, and it runs.

The key to any learning is to have a goal and then understand the pieces that must be mastered to reach your goal. By knowing and understanding what is going to happen on and off the court, both you and your partner will be able to achieve greater success at a faster rate.

THE
ELEMENTS
OF
*D*OUBLES

. . . . *M*ost people who play tennis on a nonprofessional basis play doubles, because more people can be on the court at one time. This is an important consideration if you are paying court fees or when the number of available courts is limited. Most adult recreational leagues play doubles for the same reasons. Also, as aging and conditioning become factors, more people turn to doubles. Doubles can be nearly as intense a workout as singles, even though you have a partner with whom you share the serving and re-turning duties.

For children who are serious about competing at a high level, learning to play doubles is crucial, since all high school and college teams play doubles matches. I tell my junior players to look at the draw when they are playing a tournament to see whether they can find someone from their area to team up with. When I was a junior player many years ago, I played for three years with Kevin Conway, and we never lost a match. We continued to play together in college at

Wisconsin, and the junior doubles experience definitely made us better college doubles players.

At the pro level, most tournaments include doubles events. Many pros are doubles specialists, though a few of the top-ranked players save their energy for singles only. Some pros use doubles as a way to practice their singles game. Because there is less pressure to chase down every ball, it is not uncommon for the pros to take advantage of the light workout on off days. And what better way to practice skills than playing doubles? This is the strategy John McEnroe used. As he explained it, doubles enabled him to practice all his skills to stay sharp for his next singles match.

Most junior and adult tournaments include doubles events for men and women, and there are leagues for men's, women's, and mixed doubles play at all levels. Because most adults who play tennis play doubles, the recreational tennis leagues focus primarily on doubles. The key to being a good doubles team is finding a partner with whom you enjoy playing. A doubles partnership is like any other partnership; some teams work well together, and others do not. Of course, playing repetitively with the same partner helps the team learn to function better as a unit.

THE DOUBLES COURT

*B*oth singles and doubles tennis is played on a court that is 78 feet long and divided horizontally in the middle by a net. Thus each side has 39 feet of hitting length. The singles court is 27 feet wide. The doubles court expands 4.5 feet on each side to 36 feet. The expansion area is called the alley. The net height should always be 3 feet in the middle of the court, 3 feet 6 inches on the sidelines.

THE FOUR PLAYERS

*T*here are four players on the doubles court: Player A, the server; Player B, the server's partner; Player C, the serve returner; and Player D, the serve returner's partner. Each player occupies a certain spot on the court, and each of these spots carries with it specific responsibilities. In doubles, one partner is responsible for the right half

The four basic positions

of the court and the other is responsible for the left. There are times, which will be discussed later, when the players change responsibilities, but basically each partner is responsible for a side. The division is *not* up and back; it is left or right.

BASIC POSITIONS

- *Server's position: in the middle of the side the player is responsible for, behind the baseline.*

- *Server's partner's position: in the middle of the side the player is responsible for on the ⅝ line. To find this spot, divide the area between the net and the service line in half, then take one small step back toward the service line.*

- *Serve returner's position: near the singles out-of-bounds line around the baseline area.*

- *Serve returner's partner's position: ⅝ line in the middle of the player's area of responsibility. (A less experienced player should stand on the service line in the middle of his or her area of responsibility.)*

ELEMENTS YOUR TEAM MUST RESOLVE

Who Plays Which Side?

Neither side is easier or tougher to return serve from. When you play singles, you return from both sides. In doubles, however, it is not unusual for a player to prefer one side, usually the forehand. Because many inexperienced players fear their backhands, they want to play only the forehand side of the court, commonly referred to as the deuce court. But what they don't realize is that by moving out one more step, the returner will actually hit more backhands at a higher level than in the backhand or "ad" court. To facilitate the backhand crosscourt return, you should move out one step toward the alley so that you can get an exaggerated turning of your lead hip toward your crosscourt hit location.

You and your partner must work out who plays which side. In practice, change around to see what works best for your team. Often when you are playing team or league matches, you will be teamed with an unfamiliar partner or someone who prefers the same side of the court as you. Since someone has to play the nonfamiliar side, avoid this problem by practicing both sides.

If you lose the first set, it is usually not a good idea to change returning sides. Instead of focusing on which side you are playing or not playing, focus more on the ball. See the stroker hit the ball; watch the path of your opponent's racquet and the direction of the incoming ball.

The only time it might be worthwhile to change sides is when you and your partner feel that you were outmatched from the onset. Usually, though, both of you simply need to track the ball better.

Who Serves First?

Usually the stronger server serves first, because in a 6–4 set, the stronger server serves three times, his or her partner twice. If sun and wind conditions are factors and one player has a weaker serve, then that player should be the one serving into the wind. Don't diminish the stronger partner's strength by having that player serve into the wind; otherwise, the team ends up with two weak servers.

In doubles, the serve rotates between the teams. Player A serves, then Player C. Next Player A's partner serves, followed by Player C's partner. This rotation is maintained throughout the set. When the set is over, each team may set a new rotation order for itself. It behooves the team to have its stronger server start each new set. Thus, if Player C served the second, sixth, and tenth games of set one, which her team won 6–4, she may serve her team's first game of the new set. Assuming that her team wins again 6–4, Player C will have served six times and her partner four. A new serving rotation may be a big advantage.

Many players like to receive the first game because it gives them one game to get into the match before going on the offensive with the serve. Most big servers prefer to start serving because they believe that it gives them a psychological advantage and keeps them on the offensive. One reason for choosing side first would be to hit with the wind rather than into it for two of the first three games or not to serve into the sun on your first service game.

TIEBREAKERS

The tiebreaker in doubles is similar to the regular service rotation. Player A serves one point, then the teams rotate servers every two points. Six points are played before the teams switch sides. The teams change sides after each additional sixth point, which leads to one or more of the servers serving on a different side. When the sun and wind are factors in the match, this change requires additional focus and mental toughness. The first team to win seven or more points by a two-point margin wins the set.

· · ·
THE WARM-UP

*B*efore the match starts, players warm up with each other for a short time. At tournament-level play, only 5 minutes is allowed before play must begin. Tour players have warmed up extensively elsewhere and use this time as the final warm-up.

Ready Your Shots for Play

Unfortunately, many novice players do not understand the intent of the warm-up, which is to quickly ready your shots for the play about to begin. Too often, players use the warm-up period inappropriately to practice put-away shots, or they hit poorly on purpose to throw off the opponent. Occasionally, a player simply cannot hit the ball back. All three lead to no warm-up for either player. Each player is obligated to warm up the opponent and should be hitting the shots back with moderate to good speed.

A player should warm up all the skills—strokes, volleys, serves, and overheads—before play begins. Although many new players like to delay practicing the serve until it is their turn in the match, this is not allowed. Since play must be continuous once the game has begun, players should hit two or three serves, then let the opponent hit two or three during the warm-up. If a server continues to hit practice serves into the net, he or she should return the balls across the net instead of continually trying to make serve. Otherwise the opponent will have no time to warm up his or her serve. This is unfair and is not allowed.

The warm-up is the place to set the tone of the match. As a player, you are out there to compete, not to be a jerk. Never try to aggravate your opponent before the match starts, or you'll be burdened with a contentious, rancorous match where time seems to inch by.

I tell all my players that they must do a full half hour warm-up before they go into their matches. This way, the match warm-up is really unnecessary. If you use the first set as a warm-up, you will always be down in the score and risk giving your opponents an unstoppable momentum. If your opponents can't or will not warm you up, that becomes their problem; you will still be ready to play.

...
DOUBLES ETIQUETTE

Clearing the Court

When you are the net player and your serving partner's first serve goes into the net, clear the ball off the court. Let the server stay focused on the serve rhythm and not be distracted by the loose ball.

Communication

In doubles, you and your partner are allowed to communicate during the point when the ball is on your side of the net. Calling "Yours" or "I've got it" is a good idea to make sure that you both know who is to hit the ball. Because the nonhitter often has a better view of the shot and can determine whether the ball will land in or out, that player should yell, "Bounce it" or "No." And don't forget to yell "Get back" when you've hit a poor shot, such as a short lob, that may hurt your partner. But you must speak quickly. If you wait until your opponent is ready to hit and then bark instructions, you have crossed the line of proper communication. Your opponents may claim distraction, which causes you to forfeit the point.

Crashing Racquets

If both players go for the ball and crash racquets, the play is legal as long as only one racquet hits the ball. However, if Player A nicks the ball and on the deflection Player B hits it over the net, it is a double hit, and that team loses the point.

Line Calls

All lines are good; if any part of the ball touches any part of the line, the ball continues to be played. The farther away you are from a ball, the more difficult it is to judge it correctly. Because of parallax—the apparent displacement of an object as seen from two different points—many balls that land close to the lines may appear to be out but are in reality in. When I am at the net and turn to make a baseline call, I know from experience that even though the ball appears to land on the outside color of the court, unless I see the ball out by at least 4 inches, it actually landed inside the court.

Be generous with your line calls. Keep in mind that when you are playing a match, your opponents are trying to beat you. If you make them feel that you are calling the lines incorrectly, you are only giving them extra incentive to beat you. In most cases, if you call the lines liberally, your opponents will reciprocate.

WHEN YOU AND YOUR PARTNER SEE THE BALL DIFFERENTLY

Both partners are responsible for line calls on their side of the net; however, the person closer to the line has the easier call. Still, one question that comes up all the time is what to do when you and your partner see the ball differently. I tell my students that if one partner sees the ball in, it must be called good. It does no good to throw a fit and wonder how your partner could question your integrity or not support you. Remember that you are simply calling a tennis shot. If you lose track of this and let your ego get in the way, you will be a poor partner.

Under no circumstances should you condone an inaccurate line call by your partner. In a recent match, a player mentioned to her opponents that she was embarrassed by her partner's poor line calls. But since she did not overrule her partner, those bad line calls became her bad line calls as well.

Once, to test the importance of correct line calls, my friends Steve and Greg played two sets. In the first set, Steve called all close balls out; Greg did the same in the second set. The player who was allowed to make incorrect calls won both times by the same score, 6–1.

WHAT TO DO WHEN YOUR OPPONENT CHALLENGES YOUR LINE CALL

If both you and your partner are dead sure, stick to your call. But if the ball landed close to the line, perhaps your opponents had a better view of the landing of the shot. My partner and I usually say, "We saw it out, but if you saw it in, take the point." In the four years that Mark and I have been playing together, we have been questioned only twice—and one time was when we played a ball that the opponents thought was out! If in doubt, err in your opponents' favor.

This brings up another point. Call close balls in, particularly on fast serves. Without the Cyclops machine, which automatically calls lines, it is too tough to call a close serve out. Although the hitting team often has a better view of the ball's landing (which may appear to be out), you must always be ready to play the ball in case the opponents call it good and continue play.

WHAT TO DO WHEN THE OPPONENTS MAKE INCORRECT LINE CALLS

Everyone misses a call now and then. However, once your opponents have missed more than two calls, you must bring the situation under control for two reasons. First, it is easy to become upset when you feel cheated; then your focus becomes weak and the team falls apart. Second, it is tough to play when the lines are "floating." If you are fearful of hitting your shots because they may land too close to the line and be called out, you will start to hold back, which means that you are coming off your game. Do not allow this to happen. In one doubles match, a friend of mine jumped over the net after another bad line call and persuasively argued against any future marginal or bad line calls. This extreme measure is not recommended!

If the line calls are in question, ask for help with the lines after two disputes. If you are playing in a tournament, ask for a linesperson. If you are playing a league match, ask the captains of the teams to send an impartial observer from each team. If you are playing with a friend whose vision is suspect or who is a deliberate cheater, consider searching for a different friend!

- *When playing a league match: Politely ask your opponents to request that their captain—and you request yours—get a linesperson because you disagree about the lines.*

- *When playing a tournament: Politely tell your opponents that you must get the tournament director because you are having a disagreement about the lines. The tournament director will send a linesperson.*

- *When playing a friendly match: If your friend constantly makes bad line calls, find a new friend to play with.*

More Points of Etiquette

➤ Tennis is a civilized sport that emphasizes fairness and politeness.

➤ Leave balls on the baseline near the center mark when changing ends, unless your side will be serving next.

➤ Do not return "fault" service balls. Let them pass to the back wall.

➤ Do not talk when your opponent is ready to hit the ball.

➤ If a ball from another court rolls onto your court during your opponent's service motion or at any other time, offer to play a let.

➤ Always call the score before each service point and the game score at the beginning of each game.

Which Side?

To determine who serves, the pros flip a coin. For everyone else, one player spins a racquet. Each racquet has a distinctive up and down side. For instance, when using a Wilson racquet, a player calls "M" or "W," since the grip handle endpiece has a *W* on it for Wilson. The winner of this spin can choose to either serve or return, specify a side and place the burden of deciding to serve or receive on the opponent, or let the opponent choose first.

Other Rules of the Game

There are a few quirky rules of the game you should know about:

➤ A ball is not out until it is called out.

➤ If the ball hits any part of your body, regardless of whether you are standing inside or outside the court, the point automatically belongs to your opponent. Thus, if the ball is clearly long and you catch it on a fly, you lose the point! Do not touch an out ball until it has bounced and been called out. The rules anticipate a hurricane occurring and blowing the ball back into the tennis court. Even if you are diligently trying to avoid being hit but the ball nicks your foot, you have lost the point. This also applies to the serve. It cannot hit you or your partner before it bounces out.

➤ You must use your racquet to hit the ball over the net. Once I was chasing a low ball in a match and just missed it, though it did hit my foot and go over the net. Although my opponent thought that I had hit the ball with my racquet, I was obligated to inform him that it was his point. You can use any part of the racquet to hit the ball. The standard response when the ball hits the edge and goes over is, "I paid for the whole racquet, therefore I plan to use the whole racquet."

➤ You can hit the ball only once on your side. There is a very thin line between a "carry," in which the shot is one continuous motion but the ball rolls on your racquet and gets thrown over the net like a jai alai shot, and a double hit, in which the ball leaves the racquet and you contact it again before it crosses the net.

➤ You are not allowed to touch the net with your racquet or any part of your body or clothing until the ball has bounced twice. If you do so, the point is over, no matter how clear it is that your shot was unreturnable.

➤ If you touch the net or reach over it, or the ball hits any part of your body or double bounces, you are obligated to call these infractions against yourself immediately. If you suspect that this has occurred with your opponent, continue to play the point. At its conclusion, ask whether the ball bounced twice or mention that a piece of clothing or body part hit the net. Because these are self-made calls, the ultimate determiner is the offending player's integrity.

(cont'd.)

➤ You must let the ball cross over the net before you hit it; you must not prohibit the ball from reaching your side.

➤ Every once in a while, due to spin or the wind, the ball lands on your side and then spins or blows back over the net before you can touch it. Once the ball has landed on your side, you can reach over the net to hit it (the only time this is permissible), as long as you do not touch the net. Unless you touch the ball, you lose the point, because it is deemed that you are not responsible for its return.

➤ If the ball you hit touches anything on or over the court, you are deemed to have missed. Thus, if there are electrical wires or lights overhead and the ball hits them, you lose the point. The only thing that can be hit is the net post, which is deemed part of the court. (I have never seen this happen.) However, if a very wide shot is returned by going around the net rather than over it, this is legal.

DOUBLES—THE SOCIAL GAME

One Sunday many years ago, when I had first started seeing my wife Karen, we were invited to play mixed doubles with another couple at their club. Upon arriving, Karen was astounded to see so many husbands interacting with their wives. Doubles tennis is a great way to socialize, both with your spouse or significant other and with other couples. We have met some of our best friends through tennis, and playing tennis with them continues to be a significant part of these friendships. In fact, we often travel to tennis tournaments with many of these same couples. We all enjoy watching and playing tennis and find that it's a great way to spend time together.

The Unwritten Rules

When you play social tennis, there are unwritten rules of behavior. For example, if all the players are of equal ability, everyone can play full-out. But when one or more players are substantially better, the better players must tone down.

Some players have difficulty adjusting to social tennis; they mistakenly believe that toning down their power destroys their game, but this isn't correct. Think of tennis as having three buttons: a try button, a focus button, and a power button. Adjust only the power button in social tennis. Don't confuse toning down your game with less focus or effort.

Recently, one of my students told me that she and her husband went to a tennis party. They were beating another couple, when suddenly the husband went ballistic. He was playing life-or-death tennis—going nuts every time he or his wife missed a shot. My student's team won that set, but when it was over, Mr. X sought out the best available female partner at the party to seek revenge. My student felt stuck, so she and her husband halfheartedly played another set, but they couldn't wait to walk off the court. Mr. X had broken the social contract—there is a place to play life-or-death tennis and a place to play social tennis.

Life-or-death tennis should be reserved for tournaments; if you play with such intensity in social situations, you are out of line. When I play tennis with my wife, I am trying to help her improve her game. I view this time as her time, not mine. I am still focused and still trying, but this is not the time or place for me to work on my competitive tennis. I will play mixed doubles with a couple only when the fellow is my equal and we both stay toned down, or when everyone is my wife's equal. Then I play as if I am giving a lesson—I just keep the ball in play and let everyone hit.

THE
*P*LAYERS

. . . . *A*s mentioned in Chapter 1, the four players on a doubles court are labeled Players A, B, C, and D. In this chapter, the basic moves each player can expect to make are discussed.

. . .
PLAYER A:
THE SERVER

*T*he server stands behind the baseline near the middle of his or her side of the court and must choose beforehand whether to serve and volley (move in toward the net) or serve and stay back.

Serving and Volleying

Before the serve is struck, the server must decide whether to go in or not. You cannot wait to judge the quality of the serve and then decide to serve and volley, because by the time you make up your mind to move, the ball will be on your side again.

Toss the ball up and in front of you. Your serve momentum must carry you forward into the court to aid in your rushing the net. If your toss is off to the side or behind you, you will never recover your balance in time to move to the net.

When you come in to the net, your goal must be to reach at least the service line. If you can't move in this far, you become vulnerable to having your toes hit on the service return or being passed wide.

SPLIT STEP

At some point when serving and volleying, you need to perform a neutral balancing step called a *split step*. Some players like to do this when their serve lands on the other side; others make their split step just before the ball is struck by the returner. I have had the most success instructing players to get to the service line before splitting. In any case, the premise is to balance yourself so you can react to the incoming return.

The first volley should be treated as an approach shot. On the first volley, you are usually too far back from the net to hit an easy winning shot, so set the team up with a volley that goes deep to the returnee's side.

KEYS TO SERVING AND VOLLEYING

1. *Make up your mind to go in.*

2. *Sprint in.*

3. *Hit deep; your first volley is treated as an approach shot.*

4. *Join your partner at the ⅝ line by the next shot.*

Serving and Staying Back

A second choice is to serve and stay back. Like with the serve and volley, you must make up your mind to stay back before you hit the serve. You should still toss the ball out in front of you to maximize the serve, then regain your balance and retreat behind the baseline into your ground-stroke position. If you are serving well but the returns are being crushed, staying back makes good sense. If you are serving and volleying and you miss many of your volleys, consider staying back. If your serve is weak, don't force the action—stay back.

1. *Make up your mind to stay back.*

2. *Reposition yourself quickly behind the baseline.*

3. *Hit deep to deep, away from the opposing net player.*

Importance of the Serve in Doubles

Whether you are playing singles or doubles, it is important to get your first serve in the service box to put the ball in play. The first serve, at all levels, should travel more miles per hour than the second serve. Since your first serve should be your "weapon," you can inflict more damage on your opponents by getting your first serve in play. Getting your first serve in also keeps the psychological pressure off of you and on your opponents, because they then have to deal with your weapon-grade serve. The pressure reverts back to you when hitting a second serve, because if you miss again, the opponents win the point. Further, if you get your first serve in play, you cannot double-fault. In televised matches, the commentators always talk about two statistics: first serve percentage and points won when the first serve goes in. At the pro level, when the first serve goes in, the serving team wins at least 80% of the points.

Some experts suggest that the serve be hit at 75% power and with more spin in order to facilitate a higher percentage of first serves going in. This suggestion makes sense if you do not have a big serve or if there is a huge drop-off in power on your second serve; however, at the higher level, this no longer holds true. If you have a big "heater" serve and a good second serve, then go for it on the first serve. If your serve is that big, you will earn many free points. It would be senseless to diminish your power.

DOUBLE-FAULTING

Regardless of which approach to serving you subscribe to, do *not* double-fault. A double fault gives your opponents a free point. If you double-fault often, your partner will become frustrated, because there is no way he or she can help you win the point if you cannot put the ball in play. Even wimpy serves are better than no serves; you must start the point.

When Does Player A Adjust Positioning?

Player A may move around to change serve angles or facilitate better serve placement but must stay on his or her side of the court and within the court boundaries, between the center mark and the doubles alley sideline.

PLAYER B:
THE SERVER'S
PARTNER

*T*he server's partner stands in the middle of his or her half of the court at an imaginary spot called the ⅝ line. To find this line, divide the area between the net and the service line in half. Then take one small step back toward the service line. Many players like to stand too close to the alley, which inadvertently causes their partners to cover the equivalent of a singles court. The net player must cover the entire half of the court, not just the alley.

Many players also like to stand very close to the net. This invites a lob, because there is so much territory left uncovered behind them. Furthermore, standing too close to the net allows net players less reaction time, making them vulnerable to power hits. Being overly close also causes a problem for the serving partner, because the server has too much ground to cover before joining the net player.

Poaching

When the ball is hit away from the net player to the opposite side of the court, Player B, the net player, could move across the court to take this shot. This movement across the court to the other side is called poaching. Since the net player is positioned at the ⅝ line, he or she has the ability to close in on the opponent's hit and get to the ⅜ line, if not closer. By closing in like this, Player B gets an opportunity to "kill" the opposing net player. By being so close to the net, Player B also develops great angles. So whether it is a planned play on the serve or a spontaneous movement off the ongoing point, the net player is looking to take the ball all the time.

Player B changes sides either on a prearranged plan on the serve or spontaneously during an ongoing point. The purpose of Player B changing sides is to facilitate the team's offense.

SIGNALING BEFORE THE SERVE

Often, Player B will signal Player A or decide ahead of time that he or she is going to poach on a particular serve. When doing this, you should not move until the ball has landed on the returnee's side.

Then, just before the ball is struck, move as fast as you can. Remember that you have committed to the movement, since you told your partner to play the other side. You cannot change your mind or chicken out halfway across. Even if the returner is able to hit the ball behind you, it does not matter, because your partner is already covering that area.

KEYS TO POACHING

1. *On a poach, move just before the returner hits.*

2. *Run in to the net on an angle.*

3. *Bounce out to the ⅝ line.*

4. *Any time a player crosses over halfway, that player stays on this new side and the partner switches.*

POINT IN PROGRESS

Whenever the teams are playing one up and one back during a point in progress, Player B, the net player, should always be looking to poach and seize the opportunity whenever possible. Player A, the back player, then crosses to the other side. There is no signal given on poaching during an ongoing point. Player B makes this move spontaneously. The deeper the drive pushes the opposition back, the more likely that a poach opportunity will occur. This is based on straight math: The greater the distance the ball must travel, the more time the net person has to observe and go for the ball.

If the drive to the other side is short, the net player should protect his or her side, since the ball has less distance to travel, resulting in less reaction time. The range of the net player determines the pressure the opposite back player feels. The more active the net player is, the more pressure there will be to hit the ball farther crosscourt.

The net player's partner must remain focused on the incoming ball rather than be distracted by an active net person. In fact, the net player's own partner is usually the one who complains that the movement is distracting, which is nonsense. The net player must feel no pressure from the backcourt partner. It is a great break for the opposition when the back player freezes his or her own net partner. Even if the net player is missing volleys, the movement causes the other team to make more errors because of the added pressure created by poaching. In the long run, a poaching team will win more points than an inactive one.

As the net player becomes more active at the net, he or she must cover the middle shot. Even if the partner is coming to the net, the net player is still in the superior court position to grab this ball.

FAKING

An alternative to poaching, and just as important as the real thing, is faking poaching. When doing this, Player B should move just before the ball lands. This hints to the returner that you are vacating your territory, so a down-the-line return appears to be the returner's best bet. Then, as the ball is being struck, quickly return to your original position.

The purpose of both poaching and faking is to draw the return to the net person. Even when the server is coming in on the serve, the net person is in a superior volleying position. He or she can advance to the net more quickly, which creates greater angles and power opportunities. Furthermore, it takes a disciplined returner not to look up to see the opposing team's activity. This movement often leads to free points, since the returner cannot watch both the ball and you at the same time. Even if the net player makes one shot and misses one, if you add the free point to the serving team's column, the score would be two to one.

The I Formation or Australian

If you do not feel comfortable moving at the net, try changing the lineup position by playing the *I formation* or *Australian*. On the I formation, the server and the net player line up on the same side of the court in an *I*. After the serve is struck, the server—who has served from the center mark—zooms in on the serve and volley on the new side or slides over three steps on the new side if staying back. The net player may still signal and run plays.

The purpose is to disrupt the returner's rhythm, which is perfectly legal. If you never make any changes, the returner can use a single return and never worry. Increase the pressure on the returner by changing the lineup.

When Do You Move?

Start the movement at the beginning of the match. When I play, the first point is always a poaching play. This puts our opponents on notice that we will be very active at the net. Oddly enough, we have played many teams who use the signals but never move. They are waiting to see if our returns are weak enough to allow them to poach, which is seldom the case, since both Mark and I return very well. As a result, these opponents do not move. This is another example of how to take your game to the opponents. Do not react—dictate.

When Does Player B Adjust Positioning?

If Player B is faced with a returner who hits every ball weak or low, he or she needs to make a correction and move in. If faced with a nonstop lobber on the return of serve, Player B should start 4 feet closer to the service line to ensure that the lobber has a more difficult time hitting the ball over the net player's head.

...
PLAYER C: THE SERVE RETURNER

The serve returner is positioned around the baseline area in his or her return court. If faced with a strong serve, Player C moves back a little for better sighting and increased reaction time. When facing a weak serve, Player C moves forward to avoid hitting running returns.

Although serving is the most important skill in tennis, serve returning runs a close second. Again, if you cannot start the point, you lose. This may be difficult when facing a big server, but you must try to hit the ball over the net and into the court. Unfortunately, you cannot tell your opponent to slow down the serve so you can get more of them back. In doubles, besides having to return the serve successfully, there is the added pressure of trying to avoid the net player to protect your partner.

Two Styles of Return

THE SLICE

The slice return is executed by hitting high to low on the ball and then driving out with the racquet. I like to call this a "slide and drive" shot, because that is the required motion. This is not a weak shot, but an offensive one. Television announcers often refer to this shot as a "chip and charge" shot, but I dislike that terminology, because chip implies a chopping down motion, which you must be careful not to do.

The slice return is a good one to use when the server stays back. The ball stays low after it lands, forcing the server to hit up on the next shot. The slice return is also a good shot to use if the server moves toward the net, because it is easy to keep the return low, driving the ball to the toes of the incoming server to make him or her volley up.

THE TOPSPIN

The second style of return is the "big-bang hit." If the server is going to whack the ball, then so will you—power on power. This shot is hit with topspin, going low to high on the ball. This is a good return to use if the server stays back, because your power can overrun the server. This is also a good return if the server follows the serve to the net, for the same reason. During a recent Davis Cup match, I could hear, via satellite, the captains coaching their teams. One captain told his players to go for the high percentage play and tone down the power to get the return in, and the other captain was advocating the opposite, telling his players to keep on banging! The one catch to the big-bang theory is that if the serve is coming in at 100+ miles per hour and the return is at equal speed, it is nearly impossible for the returner to follow that return to the net.

Both methods of return are valid. When I play, I usually use the "bang" on the first serve and the "slide and drive" on the second, always remembering that the return has to go over the net and stay within the court boundaries. Your team must play the point. If you miss too many serve returns, you make the opponents' task of holding serve too easy.

Returning Serve and Coming to the Net

Before the serve is struck, the returner must decide whether to rush the net. If you wait to make a quality judgment, it will be too late to move in as far as the service line. Instead, you must attack the serve and treat it like an approach shot—ideally hitting 2 to 4 feet inside the baseline. If you do not reach the service line, you will be vulnerable to having your toes hit or being passed wide. So attack the serve using either method of return, but remember to make up your mind and stay committed.

When the server hits the ball, do a split step so that you are balanced and can reach every possible area in which the ball might be hit.

KEYS TO RETURNING SERVE AND VOLLEYING

1. *Before the server begins the service motion, make up your mind to go in.*

2. *Pick your target and, ideally, hit it.*

3. *Try to get to the ⅝ line.*

Returning Serve and Staying Back

You also must make up your mind before you hit the return if you are going to stay back. If the incoming serve is strong, don't force coming in. If you are not getting in far enough or missing too many volleys, don't force the issue. Stay back and let the point develop. After you hit your return, quickly assume your stroke posture behind the baseline.

KEYS TO RETURNING SERVE AND STAYING BACK

1. *Make up your mind to stay back.*

2. *Pick your target and, ideally, hit it.*

3. *Reposition behind the baseline.*

When Does Player C Adjust Positioning?

Player C's moves are based on the reality of the server. The sooner in the match that Player C can ascertain the server's patterns the better he or she will be able to adjust. Then the server may adjust to Player C's adjustments, making the maneuvering similar to that in a chess match, each player moving and countering. Player C can move back if the serve is fast or move in if it's weak. To counter a serve breaking wide due to heavy spin, Player C may also move up.

PLAYER D: THE RETURNER'S PARTNER

*T*he returner's partner stands at the net in the middle of his or her half of the court, ideally at the ⅝ line, the basic volley position. Some players like to stand farther back around the service line. If you do this, make sure as the point progresses that you return to the ⅝ line. As with the server's partner, sometimes the returner's partner stands too close to the alley, which inadvertently causes the partner to cover the equivalent of a singles court. The net player must cover the entire half of the court, not just the alley.

When Does Player D Poach?

Player D is looking to move off the shot that Player A hits. If Player A's volley or stroke goes in the middle of the court between Players C and D, Player D should be aggressive and get this ball. Player D is also looking to poach if Player A's shot floats up. By trying to volley this shot, Player D is playing offensively.

KEYS TO MOVEMENT BY PLAYER D
1. *Look to intercept every ball that is hit.*
2. *Move in on an angle for the shot.*

When Does Player D Adjust Positioning?

Player D moves back to the baseline when:

❶ The return is constantly hit to the opposite net player, who nonstop kills Player D.

❷ Player C continually misses the return. Tell your partner that you will move back so he or she can aim in the middle of the court to make the return and need not worry about protecting you.

❸ The opposing net player is a great and successful poacher. By moving back, you eliminate the point-blank target.

THE PARTNERSHIP

. . . . ven though you and your partner may be good players, you may not make a good team. Some
teams work well together; others never do. At the pro level, partner-
ships change all the time. The most successful women's team ever was
Pam Shriver and Martina Navratilova. They stopped playing together
after many years, feeling that the team had grown stale. On the men's
side, it was said that the best doubles team was John McEnroe and
whoever was his current partner.

PICKING A PARTNER

he key to playing good doubles is having a good partner—being
a good singles player does not guarantee being a good doubles player.
When choosing a partner, look for someone who has good skills that
complement yours, because a good team is a balanced team. A few

years ago, Mark and I played a team in which one player was the best player on the court, but his partner was the weakest. We killed them!

Mark and I have commensurate skills, and we both take responsibility for controlling play. When a team has a noticeably superior player, the better player feels pressured to do more than his share, and the weaker player defers to his partner, becoming too passive. Thus a team with balanced skills is often far more successful than an unbalanced team. So when selecting a partner, do not necessarily look for a great player; look for someone on your level who will complement your game.

Another thing to look for when choosing a partner is someone who complements your philosophy. Many times, teams split because the players have different goals or a mismatched competitive spirit. This is probably the most common complaint I hear from players. If a player is very competitive, she expects the same intensity from her partner. If her partner is not as fiercely competitive in the battle, the more competitive player feels that she is carrying the entire load. And often the less competitive player feels that her partner is pressuring her too much.

There is no right or wrong level of competitiveness, but compatibility on this issue is essential if you want an enduring partnership. Whether you and your partner play life-or-death tennis in a tournament environment or play tennis only to socialize, it is critical that you share the same philosophy.

When Mark and I play tournaments, it is important to both of us that we do well and play our best. We both play with a high degree of competitiveness, energy, and intensity. As Richey Reneberg said in the foreword about helping each other out and picking each other up on occasion, our team can do this.

...
PARTNER
COMBINATIONS

At a high level of play, it is important that both partners possess all the necessary skills and can play aggressively. At the U.S. Tennis Association (USTA) 3.5 level (the USTA has created a 1–7 classification system for tennis talent; see Appendix A), many teams try to blend two diverse play styles: a steady player with an aggressive player, one responsible for setting up the point and the other for finishing it off. This makes for a tough combination to play against, because the two styles never give the opponents a chance to find their groove or get a good hitting rhythm. However, once you clear the 3.5 level of play, if you fall short on skills, your opponents will exploit the weakness.

WORKING TOGETHER

*I*n order to achieve successful teamwork, you and your partner must be comfortable with each other's style of play, and the best way to become comfortable is to practice together. As you and your partner work together, you learn more about each other and become increasingly familiar with what works best for you as a team. I hope that you are both studying this book and working harmoniously on your play program.

Also, as with any activity that involves two people, learning to get along with your partner enables you to maximize your level of play. The secret is for each player to be responsible for carrying his or her share of the load.

HOW TO HELP YOUR PARTNER

Play Well Yourself

The best way to play well yourself is to have a good definition of all your shots. You must have a video of the shot in your mind; then you simply push the execute button when you hit. Everyone misses now and then. It is critical, however, that you do not let your arm's failure erase the video of the correct way to hit your shots.

The better you play, the easier it is for your partner to play better. During one of my tournaments, I observed a good doubles match in which all four players were quite good, but one player was having a tough time on the serve return. Finally his partner turned to him and said, "I can't do this by myself. You must help." If you go into a miss mode, your partner inevitably feels that every time he hits the ball he must win the point, which is an impossible task. The pressure created is too immense; your partner ends up trying too hard, which results in his performing poorly. You must hold up your end of the partnership to help out your partner.

Have a Good Doubles Attitude

In doubles, it is easy not to be intensely focused because you are not hitting every ball—you are sharing them with your partner. But you must develop a doubles attitude wherein you expect that every ball is going to come to you. This will make you constantly ready and in the point. Further, you must want every ball to come to you. This is not an insult to your partner, but simply a good doubles attitude. If you are looking for the ball and wanting to play the ball, you will play more aggressively and cover more of the shots.

Run the Plays

When you play, you and your partner must be on the same page of the playbook. If your partner comes in but you suddenly retreat, you distract your partner. Instead of focusing on the ball, he will be wondering where you are going and why.

I am a very good doubles player. At a tournament years ago, a player ranked above me in singles asked if I would play with him because his partner had to withdraw. Knowing that he was a good singles player, I welcomed the opportunity. (I pointed out earlier that playing singles well does not guarantee a good doubles player.) I was surprised that he was such a weak doubles player—most of the match I was looking around for him, trying to figure out where he was going. Obviously we were not on the same page of the playbook. As a result of this distraction, my play suffered greatly because I could no longer focus on me and the ball. We lost.

Sometimes you and a new partner are immediately comfortable. Other times, you never seem to be in sync or able to work things out. But either way, make sure that you are not the one compromising the team.

Be Ready

You must ready yourself before the point starts and stay ready throughout the point. I mention this again and again because it is so important. If I see my partner acting like a lump, I am distracted and cannot focus on the ball. I want to yell to my opponents not to start play because when my partner is not ready, I am not ready. Even if you are the server's partner or the serve returner's partner and the earliest ball you can hit is ball three or four, you must be ready for action before the first ball is struck. To do otherwise ensures a losing strategy and is disrespectful of your partner.

Trust Your Partner

You must trust your partner to take care of his or her shots and side. If you are constantly hogging the court, your partner will become court shy and let balls go through because he or she automatically expects you to take them. As you squeeze your partner's court down, he or she begins to play much worse, never being certain when to hit the ball.

One further word of caution here: Recently one of my students played with an overly aggressive partner. During her next clinic, I noticed that she was not covering shots that were clearly hers. Just because Ms. X hogs all the shots when she is your partner, this does not mean that all your other partners will do the same. You must be careful not to let yourself become a universally small-ground coverage player because of one partner.

Talk

To work together as a team, you and your partner must talk. Learn what to say to your partner to help him or her function better. One of my students always encourages her partner by yelling "Run, run, run" for the deep lobs or drop shots, or "Swing" on balls that require a long stretch. Some partners like this; others don't. Know which your partner prefers. Often the nonhitter has a better read on a shot and can bark the proper command.

Recently one of my students told me that when he plays mixed doubles and his wife barks commands, he just freezes. He is distracted by her. You and your partner must figure out what you can say to each other. When I tell Mark to get his first serve in, it is a reminder of the task to be accomplished and what to focus on. I am not belittling or denigrating him, but simply trying to encourage him.

Do Not Coach Your Partner

If your partner asks what he or she is doing wrong and you have observed something, then by all means share your observation—briefly. Remember, however, that very few partners respond well to being coached on every point. They may perceive you as a know-it-all and think that you are blaming them for the misses in the match. What you say and how you say it may make the team hold together or fall apart.

Be open to adjustments. Both players need to try to spot trends in the match. If your partner makes a suggestion, be open to trying different things. The key to remember is: Do not change a winning game, but learn to make adjustments if you are losing.

Learn to Return from Both Sides

When you play singles, you practice returning from both sides. But many players who play only doubles learn to return serve well from only one side, even though neither side is more difficult to play. If you play only one side, you limit your possible play partners, because switching sides will be too difficult for you. Therefore, it's a good idea to mix up the sides on which you play.

When you play a match, you need to decide which sides you and your partner will play. I believe that changing sides during a match is one of the least productive changes. However, if you are getting rolled and have no apparent chance of winning, why not?

Do Not Quit on Your Partner

Even if your partner is having an unbelievably bad day, try your best to keep the team going. If you play well and hang in there, it is possible that your partner will come around. Your partner feels pressure from the opponents, but if he or she feels pressured by you as well, your partner's play may never stabilize. Good teams help each other through the rough patches.

Be Technologically Current

In tennis, racquet technology changes radically and frequently. Don't be technologically inadequate. If your team is playing with old technology when your opponents have the latest weapons, you are giving them at least a 10% advantage. If you are a serious player, you need a serious racquet—a wide-body racquet. You don't necessarily need the latest racquet or the widest racquet made, but you do need a racquet that is technologically current.

...
KEEPING THE TEAM IN SYNC

Before and during the match, a good team needs to make sure that both members are in sync that day. There are three things you must do to ensure this. First, before the match, you and your partner must sit down with each other and formulate your *game plan*. Next, you must develop *match analytical skills*. Then you must *huddle* or communicate.

The Game Plan

You need to plot the strategy your team will use. When the San Francisco Forty-niners football team plays a game, they run their first 15 plays the way they were scripted, which is what you should do in your match. Walk onto the court committed to your predetermined game plan.

Although some pros admit to not having a game plan, very few players wait to see how their opponents are playing before implementing a game plan. Of course, you may need to adjust your plan once you've given it every opportunity to work, but to start play without a plan is a poor strategy. Why deliberately plan to play reactive tennis? Reactive tennis reflects a negative and defensive posture.

In their Super Bowl performances, the Denver Broncos were never able to figure out how to stop the opposition. Don't make the same mistake. Walk onto the court planning to play aggressively and make your opponents stop you. And only if they stop you cold do you adjust your game plan.

You should always discuss the following with your partner:

❶ Are we going to serve and come in or not?

❷ Are we going to return serve and come in or stay back?

❸ Who covers the middle?

❹ Who covers the short balls?

❺ Who chases down the lobs?

❻ How do we switch?

I hope that you and your partner study the play section in this book and agree on how you are going to play your match beforehand.

Match Analytical Skills

Your team needs to develop match analytical skills. Both you and your partner must keep your eyes wide open and your computers turned on. Even though your game plan may be working, you still need to fine-tune your program to the reality of the day's opponents. Some of the things you must observe include:

❶ Which hand do they hit with? Inexperienced players are often so focused on their own play that they fail to observe the most obvious. The spin delivered by a right-handed hitter is different from that delivered by a left-hander. Also, at the beginner level, the backhand side is often the opponent's weaker side. Thus, knowing which side is the opponent's backhand side is important.

❷ How do today's conditions affect you and your opponents? What is the sun's position? From which direction is the wind blowing? What is the court speed?

❸ What is the quality of your opponents' shots, spin, and placement? You should have a full scouting report on them by the third game. It is important that partners share and discuss this information and that both are receptive to the information. If your partner tells you to watch the short-angle service return because it has happened three straight times, it is important that you respond favorably. Furthermore, you need to continue to observe and communicate throughout the match.

In one tournament, my partner and I had determined that Player D had the weaker overhead. I made a great scramble switch and threw up a lob to Player C. My partner half kiddingly, half seriously said, "If you're going to make such a great get, lob to the right player." He was right; for a moment I just forgot to whom I should hit the ball.

You need to remind each other about who is the stronger player, who is the stronger server, where the sun is, from which direction the wind blows. A good team continually communicates and reminds each other of the seemingly obvious. Do not assume that because you are knowledgeable about these things your partner is also as observant.

Huddling

A good team communicates, huddling after each point. If you watch any pro doubles match, you will see both teams huddle for a moment after every point. I call these "formula huddles." For example:

> ➤ *Serve side formula*: Server gets his first serve in; the net player is active.

> ➤ *Serve return side formula*: Call your return (cross-court or down the line) and tell your partner if you are coming in or staying back.

The purpose of the huddle is to go over the game plan and make a commitment to play the next point. This interaction helps the team work together. If you blow a shot, apologize and get on with it. You are allowed only 20 seconds between points, so get together to set the plan for the next point.

Remember, if you give your best effort each time you play, your partner will be encouraged to put forth his or her best effort too. A successful partnership is mutually encouraging and supportive.

KEEPING THE TEAM IN SYNC
1. *Have a game plan.*
2. *Develop match analytical skills.*
3. *Huddle.*

DOUBLES STRATEGY

. . . . *O*nce a player is able to stroke with some consistency and play at the net fairly aggressively, usually around the 3.5 level and up, the team that can control the net is going to win most of the matches. The key concept to winning requires you and your partner to form a "wall" at the net.

. . .
THE WALL

*T*he foremost way to put pressure on your opponents is to position yourselves at the net on an imaginary line at the ⅝ spot. On paper, the net team is unbeatable at this spot. Any ball that Player C, the returner, hits has to flow through an area that is reachable by either Player A or Player B at the net.

➤ If Player C hits down Player B's alley, Player B can cross over to get it.

➤ If Player C tries to power crosscourt, Player A can cross over to get it.

➤ If Player C powers down the middle, both Players A and B can cover the shot.

➤ If Player C tries to power the ball through either Player A or Player B, either player can step sideways to handle the shot.

➤ If Player C tries a dip shot to either player, the player can charge the shot and hit it.

➤ If Player C tries to lob to either player, the player can go back and hit a power overhead shot.

Remember that once the wall is in place, the team at the net must inflict damage by either powering near the net player or short-angling the deep player. To execute a power volley, the volleyer sets the racquet at a left or right 90-degree angle and drives through the shot. When angle volleying, the volleyer places the racquet head at a 60- or 110-degree angle and touches the ball with the racquet. Occasionally Player C will be able to outexecute the wall, but at a high level of play, the net team will win 75% of the points.

KEYS TO THE WALL
1. *Use your feet to cover the ground you are supposed to.*
2. *Do "damage" to the ball.*

DAMAGE

Mean Drill

When one of the players at the net receives the ball, it is that player's job to do damage with that shot by powering around the closer opponent. I call this being "mean" because it is mean to hit at or around the opposing net person, but being mean is really just correct ball placement. It is not a matter of which opponent is the weaker player, but mathematics. Who has fewer seconds to react and less distance to track the ball? The answer is the close opposite net player, so try to hit the ball around this player.

The Power Volley

The power volley is your basic volley. Start with your racquet at a left or right angle, depending on whether you are hitting a forehand or backhand; then drive outward with a punch or short quarter-circle follow-through.

The angle shot is hit by placing your racquet head at a 60-degree angle in front of your wrist to produce the out angle. The reverse angle shot is hit by placing your racquet at a 110-degree angle to your wrist.

The short-angled shot hit toward the deep opponent's (Player C's) sideline is a shot that is nearly impossible to run down. This shot becomes mandatory if the net player (Player A or B) is faced with a shot below net level. At an upper level of play, the opposite net player (Player D) is aware of the close-to-close play and will protect himself or herself. Thus, if you hit up on the ball, you are presenting the opposing net player with a seemingly floating pumpkin, and you suddenly become the target. Therefore, if a player hits a shot that dips below net level, the opposing team's response should be to return another dip shot, short-angled away from the opposing net player's sideline.

If you fail to do damage with your volley, your opponents won't fear you at the net. One of the premier women's pro doubles players is not as strong as her rating implies because she always needs more than one put-away opportunity. If I hit the ball to you at the net and you just hit it back to me, I am not threatened by your net position because of the unlimited opportunities to go around or over your team. And given enough chances, I will eventually be successful.

KEYS TO DAMAGE

1. *Power the close-to-close player.*

2. *Angle close to the net, away from the deep player.*

...
ESCAPING

*S*ometimes Players A and B will be positioned at the net, forming a wall, because Player A either served and volleyed or was invited into the net. When the opposing back player is facing that wall, he or she must try to escape by hitting through, around, under, or over the wall to keep his or her teammate at the net from getting "killed." Certain responses from you will either protect your partner or get him or her killed. The concept of protecting your partner is called *escaping*, and there are several ways to accomplish it:

➤ The back stroker can try to hit at the bodies of either net player, hoping to literally run them over.

In one of my clinics for young players, whenever one stroker would take a big windup, the opposing net player would become fearful and abandon her net spot.

➤ The stroker can try to hit a power shot toward the opposing net player's alley, hoping that this player will not have enough range to cover the shot.

➤ The stroker can power the ball between the players at the net, hoping that the net team has not worked out who will cover this shot. Often inexperienced players act like magnets that repel each other. Both players vacate the hit area, thinking that the other partner will hit them or the ball.

➤ By placing more spin on the shot or softening the hit, the stroker can hit the ball so that it dips just over the net. The net players may not be able to move fast enough or bend low enough to get to the ball, but if they do, they will be able to return only a weak, floating shot.

➤ The stroker can lob over the heads of the net team. The net players will either have poor overhead shots or be confused as to who should chase down and hit the ball.

KEYS TO ESCAPING
1. *Pick one target and do not change your mind.*
2. *Vary your shot selection so you do not become predictable.*

DEEP TO DEEP; CLOSE TO CLOSE

*F*inally, one of the keys to understanding the upcoming playbook is to remember that all doubles strategy flows from the concept that when you are deep in the court you hit the ball to the deep target, and when you are close to the net you hit the ball to the close target. Until you are positioned at or inside the net at the $5/8$ line, you are in a deep position, requiring patience and hitting back to the deep target. When you are close, power around the other net player or short-angle the deep player.

CHAPTER
5.

THE
*P*LAYBOOK

. . . . *D*uring a football game, if you watch the players on the sidelines, you often see them studying pictures that have been taken from the coaches' boxes and sent down to the players. The players are studying plays that have taken place during the game in order to develop a better understanding of how to respond to the pictured situation. I've constructed something similar here for doubles tennis. The purpose of my playbook is to help you develop a better understanding of how to respond to given situations on the doubles court.

The playbook in this chapter covers various scenarios that you may encounter on the court. These scenarios fall under four categories: the serve and serve return; a point in progress in which both sides have one player at the net and the other back; a point in progress in which one of the teams is at the net and the other is still one up and one back (in which case the back player must protect the net player by escaping out of the danger of the opponents at the net); and finally the case in which both players stay back at the baseline, or "both back."

Each scenario is followed by pictures of the doubles players responding to the given situation. In some situations, you will be shown how to go for more on the shot; in others, you will be cautioned to go for less just to stay in the point. Knowing which shot to hit and where to hit it greatly increases your chances for success because you will be aiming the ball and following through to the target area. Chasing down a tough ball with a plan in mind helps you achieve your goal.

Once you become familiar with the scenarios presented, your confidence and ability to move quickly as a team will increase. Your success in running these plays depends on good movement by the team. There are two movement clocks that your team must maximize. The first clock starts when your team hits the ball and ends when your opponent team hits the ball. Once your team has concluded the hit, every tick of this clock must be used to reposition your team in preparation for the return shot. One of your team's main goals is to learn where to reposition—to develop the ability to come off the last shot and move quickly with a purpose.

The second clock begins when the opposing team hits the ball and ends when your team hits the ball. Again, the key goal is to maximize your team's movement on every tick of this clock. The key to moving off your opponents' hit is to know what to look for: angle of

Picture 1

Picture 2

racquet at contact point, length of follow-through on the drive, and directional flow of the hit. Pictures 1 and 2 show the contact point. This will tell you the spin—whether the racquet face is open for a slice as in Picture 1, or squared up for a topspin shot as in Picture 2—and the power of the shot. If it was hit early, it was hit with more power due to better body involvement. If it was hit late, it has less power due to less body usage. When playing, you should also be able to hear the solidness of the hit. A more solid sound means more power, because the racquet strength was maximized.

Picture 3 captures the drive-through picture. The longer the drive-through, the more depth or speed on the ball. If the hitter chops down, the ball will float.

Picture 4 addresses the directional flow of the hit—whether the ball will go to the left or the right. It is critical that you never guess flow direction but *read* it. Within a foot of the ball's leaving the racquet, you should be able to discern whether it is moving right or left or straight at you.

If you can read the direction, speed, and spin of the opponent's hit, you will have time to reach the ball and control your response.

Picture 3   *Picture 4*

USING THE PLAYBOOK

*F*or each play, I set a scenario (in boldface) and follow this with directions explaining how each player is likely to respond. Your job is to understand the situation presented, then go through each play as one of the players—noting, as the play develops, your ideal reactions in combination with your partner's. This exercise should increase your knowledge of how your response to a situation will create a new situation and so on, thereby increasing your ability to react quickly and correctly on the court.

For each play, there is also a set of pictures for you to study. These should help you visualize the plays and increase your understanding of play development—what shot to hit, where to hit it, and where to go next on the court. You should soon be able to play without thinking—programmed tennis will take over, enabling you to focus on the shot itself without expending energy and time on the decision-making process.

You can mentally run through each play as many as four times, assuming the role of a different player each time. I also suggest going over these plays with your partner. The only way a team will ever do well is for it to move, react, think—essentially play—together.

KEYS TO USING THIS PLAYBOOK

1. *Identify and understand the boldface scenario.*

2. *Run through the play-by-play, assuming the identity of any one player.*

3. *Study the pictures to better understand play development.*

4. *Repeat the process, assuming different roles.*

5. *Share this information with your partner.*

6. *Put your understanding to good use through quick and correct team play on the court.*

Serve and Serve Return Plays

1 *Player A serves and volleys. Player C hits a driving crosscourt return and rushes the net.*

Player A serves and rushes the net, attempting to reach the service line. The first volley goes back crosscourt. After this shot is hit, A moves in 3 feet more to form the wall with Player B.

Player B holds her spot.

Player C, after the return, attempts to follow the return to the net. Ideally she hits her first volley from inside the service line. She can hit in any direction, as all four players are at the net. After her first shot, she moves in to join her partner.

Player D holds her spot if she started at the ⅝ line.

2 *Player A serves and rushes the net. Player C returns a drive crosscourt and stays back.*

Player A attempts to reach the service line. The first volley goes back crosscourt. After this shot is hit, A moves in 3 feet more to form the wall with Player B.

Player B holds his spot.

Player C bounces behind the baseline to prepare for A's volley. He faces the wall and must escape. His next shot is either power down his alley, power middle, short crosscourt angle, or lob.

Player D holds his spot.

3 *Player A serves and stays back. Player C rushes the net.*

Player A bounces behind the baseline to prepare for C's return. He faces the wall and must escape. His next shot is either power down his alley, power middle, short crosscourt angle, or lob.

Player B holds his spot.

Player C rushes the net, attempting to reach the ⅝ line.

Player D holds his spot.

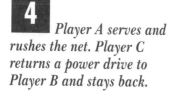

4 *Player A serves and rushes the net. Player C returns a power drive to Player B and stays back.*

Player A continues in to the ⅝ line.

Player B holds her ground, trying to power through Player D.

Player C stays back.

Player D holds her ground.

5 *Player A serves and rushes the net. Player C returns a power drive below net level to Player B and comes in behind the return.*

Player A continues in to the ⅝ line.

Player B dips the ball on a soft touch hit on the short angle away from Player C.

Player C tries for the ball.

Player D may try to chase the hit.

NOTE: For Scenarios 4 and 5, Player C may either come in or stay back. For either scenario, Player B will try the power return through Player D, known as the mean drill, if the ball is above the net. If the ball lands below the net, Player B will angle the ball back to Player C's side.

6 *Player A serves and remains behind the baseline. Player C returns high to Player B.*

Player A then rushes toward ⅝ line. (When your partner is invited to go on the offensive, you rush the net in support.)

Player B holds his ground, trying to power through Player D—the mean drill.

Player C continues in toward the net.

Player D holds his ground, trying to survive the big hit.

7 *Player A serves and remains behind the baseline. The return of serve is hit low to Player B.*

Player A then rushes toward the ⅝ line.

Player B tries to hit a dip angle short toward Player C.

Player C continues in toward the net.

Player D holds his ground, trying to survive the big hit.

8 *Player A serves and volleys. Player C lobs the return toward Player A.*

Player A stops, hits the overhead, then proceeds toward the net.

Player B starts back to cover the lob but, seeing that Player A can cover the ball, advances toward net.

Player C holds his position if Player A hits the overhead.

Player D, at the $\frac{5}{8}$ line, retreats to the baseline with his partner unless he feels brave or insulting.

9 *Player A serves and volleys. Player C lobs the return over Player A.*

Player A runs back, lets the ball bounce, then hits it.

Player B retreats to the baseline with his partner.

Player C charges toward the net.

Player D holds his position.

10 *Player A serves and stays back. Player C lobs the return toward Player A.*

Player A comes in and hits the overhead.

Player B holds his position.

Player C holds his position.

Player D holds his position.

11 *Player A serves and volleys. Player C lobs the return over Player B.*

Player A advances toward the ⅝ line if Player B hits the overhead.

Player B hits the overhead and returns to the ⅝ line.

Player C holds his position.

Player D holds his position if the ball is deep. If the lob is short, Player D retreats to the baseline.

12 *Player A serves and volleys. Player C lobs the return over Player B, who runs back, lets the ball bounce, then hits it.*

Player A retreats with her partner to the baseline.

Player B has retreated to the baseline.

Player C attacks toward the ⅝ line when the opposition retreats.

Player D holds her position.

13 *Player A serves and stays back. Player C lobs the return over Player B, who hits the overhead.*

Player A advances toward the ⅝ line.

Player B hits an overhead.

Player C holds his position.

Player D holds his position if the ball lands deep or retreats if it is short.

14 *Player A serves and stays back. Player C hits a good lob return over Player B. Player B yells, "Help."*

Player A crosses over and either hits the ball on the fly (blitzes) or lets it bounce.

Player B switches and advances on the blitz or retreats on the bounced ball.

Player C moves in toward the net.

Player D holds his position.

15 *Player A serves wide to Player C and advances toward net.*

Player A moves in toward the net, hedging toward the middle of the court.

Player B slides two steps toward the alley.

Player C returns anywhere; however, because the angle has changed, the down-the-line shot is now in his favor.

Player D slides to the middle two steps.

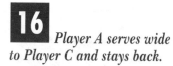

16 *Player A serves wide to Player C and stays back.*

Player A slides to the middle of the court.

Player B slides two steps toward the alley.

Player C returns anywhere; however, because the angle has changed, the down-the-line shot is now in her favor.

Player D slides to the middle two steps.

17 *Player A serves and volleys. Player C returns short and floats the ball toward Player A.*

Player A, after a split step, charges the ball, going for the win by powering the ball down the line or angling it short, back to Player C's side. Because the ball floated, Player A can use the extra time to move inside the win line, the $^5/_8$ line.

Player B holds his position.

Player C holds his position.

Player D runs for his life.

18 *Player A serves and volleys. Player C floats the ball to Player B.*

Player B attacks the ball, going for the win. He powers the ball around Player D or short-angles Player C.

Player A continues to close toward the net.

Player C holds his position.

Player D runs for his life.

Poaching Plays

During the course of a normal match, the server will often be faced with about 50 balls to hit during his or her service games. But my partner Mark and I have played doubles matches in which the server hit only two balls after the serve. Once we even played a set in which Mark never hit a ball after he served because of my movement at the net. The purpose of the movement is to draw the opponent's hit to the net player or, better yet, confuse the opponents so that they simply miss.

When I am poaching, I try to make the opponent believe that the crosscourt shot is safe, then I close it off. When I fake the poach, I try to make the opponent think that the down-the-line shot is safe, but I close it down. When we play, we have a simple formula: Get the first serve in, and the net player will do the rest.

19 *Poaching: Player A serves and volleys; Player C returns crosscourt.*

Player A should serve to the middle, take two steps in, then break to the other side and in. Player A must still get to the service line.

Player B waits until the ball has landed and Player C's head goes down to hit the ball, then sprints in on the angle, hitting either a power shot around Player D or a short angle back to Player C, then continues his movement to change sides. Player B should not return to his original spot.

Player C rushes the net or stays back.

Player D hopes for the best and holds his ground.

20

Poaching: Player A serves and stays back; Player C returns crosscourt.

Player A serves, waits one count, then breaks to the other side.

Player B waits until the ball has landed and Player C's head goes down to hit the ball, then sprints in on the angle, hitting either a power shot around Player D or a short angle back to Player C.

Player C returns crosscourt.

Player D hopes for the best and holds her ground.

21
Poaching: Player A serves and volleys; Player C returns down the line.

Player A runs over on the cross and hits the first volley deep to deep, down the line to Player C.

Player B, who crossed, bounces out to the ⅝ line.

Player C moves either up or back.

Player D must slide to the middle to close the gap.

NOTE: When Player A gets the volley, he has an easy winner in the gap area between Players C and D, unless Player D slides and squeezes the middle of the court to close the gap.

22

Poaching: Player A serves and stays back; Player C returns down the line.

Player A serves, runs over on the cross, and returns the ball deep to Player C.

Player B switches sides with Player A.

Player C remains back. If Player C comes in, Player A must escape.

Player D squeezes the middle.

23 *Poaching: Player A serves and volleys; Player C returns power middle.*

Player A serves and volleys.

Player B must reach back to cover the ball.

Player C remains back or comes in.

Player D hopes for the best and holds his ground.

24 *Player A serves and rushes the net. Player B poaches; Player C lobs over Player B.*

Player A moves in, then crosses over.

Player B must read the ball, then go back to get the ball.

Player C comes in if the lob is deep or holds his position if it is short.

Player D goes back if the lob is short or remains if the lob is deep.

25 *Player A serves and rushes the net. Player B poaches; Player C lobs to Player A.*

Player A puts on the brakes and hits the overhead.

Player B goes to the $\frac{5}{8}$ line on the new side.

Player C comes in if the lob is deep or holds his position if it is short.

Player D hopes for the best and holds his ground.

26 *Player A serves and rushes the net while Player B fakes the poach. Player C returns crosscourt.*

Player A volleys deep back to Player C.

Player B stays.

Player C may come in or stay back.

Player D holds his position.

27 *Player A serves and volleys while Player B fakes the poach. Player C sees Player B move, believes the fake, and returns down the line.*

Player A continues to the net.

Player B angles the ball to Player C or powers it toward Player D.

Player C may be in or back.

Player D squeezes the middle.

28 *Player A serves and volleys. Player C hits the return at Player A's feet.*

Player A volleys crosscourt.

Player B holds his position.

Player C crosses over.

Player D moves in on the angle and powers the ball through either player.

29 *Player A serves and volleys. Player C returns crosscourt. Player A power volleys in the middle of the court.*

Player B holds his position.

Player C is either in or back. If Player D crosses over, then C switches to D's side.

Player D picks off the ball. He is looking to move, thus the middle ball is his. Usually Player D will not go over the middle line but return to his side. Player D powers the ball at either Player A or Player B.

30 *Australian positioning: Player C returns crosscourt.*

Player A stands near the center mark, as if serving in singles. After the serve, Player A moves to the side opposite him.

Player B holds and goes for the power drive to Player D or angles to Player C.

Player C stays in or moves back.

Player D holds his position.

NOTE: If Player B fakes the poach, the same scenario is used.

31 *Australian positioning: Player C returns down the line. Player A stands near the center mark as if serving in singles, then rushes the net on the new side.*

Player A volleys straight, hitting the ball deep to deep to Player C.

Player B holds his position.

Player C stays in or moves back.

Player D squeezes the middle of the court.

32 *Australian positioning: Player B poaches, and Player C returns crosscourt. Player A stands near the center mark as if serving in singles, then rushes the net on the same side from which she served.*

Player A volleys deep to Player C.

Player B stabilizes her position.

Player C stays in or moves back.

Player D slides back to her base position.

33 *Australian positioning: Player B poaches, and Player C returns down the line.*

Player A continues in to the net.

Player B power volleys Player D or angle volleys to Player C.

Player C stays in or moves back.

Player D squeezes.

In these scenarios, neither the server nor the returner has rushed the net, so the players remain in the one up and one back position. The goal is for the deep players to hit deep to deep, but this may not always happen.

Zones for Strokes

ZONE 1 *The service square. Any ball that lands inside the service square is an invitation to come to the net. In doubles, the approach shot should go crosscourt. After you hit this shot, you go in to the net. If you have a slice shot in your repertoire, this is the weapon of choice to use as you come in.*

ZONE 2 *The next 9 feet in the court past the service line. Again, any ball that lands in this area is considered an invitation to come to the net. You attack the shot and hit crosscourt, following the shot in to the net.*

ZONE 3 *The next part of the court up to the last 6 inches. If the ball lands in this zone, you respond with a ground stroke back to the opposite deep player. You must remain patient and keep the ball alive, hitting at 75% power. Hold the baseline position.*

ZONE 4 *The last part of the court. If the ball lands this deep, you may retreat slightly, looping your response back to the deep opposite player. After this shot, you should return to the baseline position.*

The key to Zones 1 and 2 is that you must read that the opponent's shot is going to land short and move into the court to strike the shot. The key to Zones 3 and 4 is remaining patient. Stay alive, keep the ball deep, and wait for a chance to play more aggressively. Do not force the action.

Zones for Volleys

ZONE 1   *The service square on the net player's side. A shot landing in this area is always the responsibility of the player at the net. You must be able to control the area you can reach with a crossover step toward the middle of the court.*

ZONE 2   *The next 3 feet on the other side of the service line. If the ball is hit into this area, the net player should be able to reach it. If you take two quick steps in on an angle toward the net, you'll be able to cover this shot and continue your offensive posture.*

ZONE 3   *The rest of the court. If the ball is hit into this area, it is the back player's responsibility to hit the shot unless it is a slow ball that would allow the net player the time to run in four steps and intercept this ball. The only other exception occurs on the service poach, when the entire new side belongs to the net player.*

KEYS TO ONE UP, ONE BACK

1. *Hit deep to deep.*

2. *Still look to play the offense by running the zones and going to the net when you are invited to go on the offensive.*

3. *Go to the net when your partner is invited to go on the offensive.*

---

34 *ZONE 4: Player C hits the ball in the last foot of Player A's court.*

Player A retreats and lets the ball come down, then power loops the ball back crosscourt and returns to the baseline setup zone, staying back.

Player B holds his position.

Player C holds his position; if Player D poaches, he switches sides.

Player D holds his position but is looking to poach.

35 *ZONE 3: Player C hits the ball into Zone 3 to Player A. Player A tries to drive the return crosscourt, then stays back.*

Player B holds his position.

Player C holds his position; if Player D poaches, he switches sides.

Player D holds his position but is looking to poach.

36 *ZONE 2: Player C hits the ball into Zone 2 to Player A.*

Player A steps up to hit a crosscourt drive, then moves in toward the net to the ⅝ line.

Player B holds his position.

Player C holds his position.

Player D holds his position.

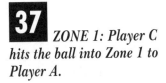

37 *ZONE 1: Player C hits the ball into Zone 1 to Player A.*

Player A hits an approach shot crosscourt, then proceeds in toward the net to the ⅝ line.

Player B holds her position.

Player C holds her position.

Player D holds her position but should be very aware of her alley.

38 *Player C hits the ball to Player B. Although this would normally be a poor shot selection, if Player B is a poor volleyer and misses the ball, it is a great choice. And if Player B is not holding his position, then hitting deep to no one is a guaranteed winner.*

Player B powers the ball around Player D or angles the ball short to Player C.

Player A charges the net, since his partner was invited to go on the offensive.

Player C holds his position.

Player D remains alert—he should be in peril.

39
Player C hits the ball low to Player B; B hits a touch shot over the net.

Players C and D both chase down the ball. If Player C calls for the ball, then Player D goes back to his side. If Player D retrieves the ball, Player C crosses over to the vacated area.

Player A charges the net, since his partner was invited to go on the offensive.

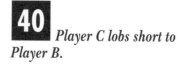 **40** *Player C lobs short to Player B.*

Player B retreats and hits the overhead.

Player A advances toward the net.

Player C holds his position.

Player D retreats to the baseline.

41 *Player C lobs deep to Player B. Player B tries to hit an overhead. If he cannot get the ball he yells, "Help." Player A then switches over.*

Player B ducks down and crosses.

Player A, after the switch, has three choices:

1. Let the ball bounce, then lob it back;

2. Let the ball bounce, then hit an overhead;

3. Attack the ball and hit it before it bounces—a blitz—then go to the net.

Player C comes in to the net if Player A responds with (1) or (2) above, but stays back if Player A blitzes.

Player D holds his position.

42 *Player C hits crosscourt to Player A; Player B poaches.*

Player B crosses over, then powers the ball around Player D or angles Player C. After the hit, Player B stays on the new side.

Player A reads that Player B has poached and switches sides.

Player C holds his position.

Player D remains alert—he should be in peril.

43 *Player C lobs to Player A. This tactic is used to stop Player B's activity at the net.*

Player A has three possible responses:

    1. Let the ball bounce, then lob back;

    2. Let the ball bounce, then hit an overhead;

    3. Attack the ball and hit it before it bounces—a blitz—then go to the net.

Player C rushes the net if Player A uses option (1) or (2).

Player B holds his position.

Player D holds his position.

The premise of this section is that the team of Players A and B has assumed the offensive net position. Player C's goal is to try to escape the dangers that the opposite team's offensive position creates. Players A and B's goal is to do damage and have an offensive, aggressive response to Player C's shot.

44 *Player C hits to Player A at the net.*

Player A hits an angle volley deep to Player C, forcing C off the court.

Players A and B move as a unit, taking two side steps in the direction of the ball, flowing with the flight path of the ball.

Player D moves as if tethered to Player C on a rope. As Player C gets pulled wide, Player D slides to the middle of the court. If Player C makes a great save, Player D then plays singles on the doubles court to give his partner time to recover and return to position.

Player C hits a power shot at Player A or B.

Player A or B, the hitter, must step to the side to avoid being jammed, then powers the ball around Player D or angles Player C.

Player B or A holds his/her position.

Player C maintains his/her position at the baseline.

Player D holds his/her position.

46 *Player C powers the ball in the middle, between the players.*

Players A and B should both go for the ball, not just the forehand player. Often the players will crash racquets, but neither the players nor the racquets will be harmed.

Player B or A holds his position.

Player C maintains his position at the baseline.

Player D holds his position.

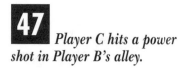 **47** *Player C hits a power shot in Player B's alley.*

Player B crosses over and powers the ball around Player D.

Player A squeezes the middle.

Player C holds his position.

Player D squeezes the gap.

Player C hits a power shot crosscourt.

Player A powers around Player D or short-angles Player C.

Player B holds his position.

Player C holds his position.

Player D hopes for the best.

49 *Player C hits a low ball to Player A.*

Player A charges the ball and hits a soft angle short to Player C.

Players C and D both chase the ball. If Player D hits the ball, then Player C switches.

Player B holds his position.

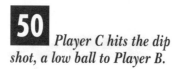

50 *Player C hits the dip shot, a low ball to Player B.*

Player B hits another dip shot on the short angle to Player C.

Players C and D both chase down the ball.

Player A holds his position.

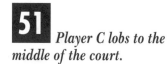

51 *Player C lobs to the middle of the court.*

Player A starts for the ball but backs off as Player B calls for the shot.

Player B goes for the overhead.

Player C stays back.

Player D holds or retreats, depending on how courageous or insulting he feels.

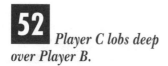

52 *Player C lobs deep over Player B.*

Players A and B both chase the ball, although the player on whose side the ball lands should cover it. Player B should hit the overhead, but if Player A can retrieve the ball, that is fine. If Player B hits the overhead, both players return to the net position.

If *Player B* must retreat and let the ball bounce, then both Players A and B return to the deep position, and Player C advances to the net.

Player D holds position.

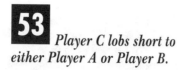 **53** *Player C lobs short to either Player A or Player B.*

The player who has been lobbed tries to hit the overhead.

Player D has time to retreat, going back to the baseline to form the deep wall.

54 *Either Player A or Player B hits the ball short to Player C.*

Player C comes in to power the ball to Player B's alley or the middle of the court, then continues to the net.

Players A and B squeeze the side on which the ball is hit by one step.

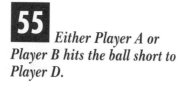

55 *Either Player A or Player B hits the ball short to Player D.*

Player D powers the ball down Player A's alley or in the middle of the court.

Player C comes to net, since his partner has taken the offensive position.

Players A and B squeeze the side on which the ball is hit by one step.

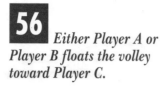

56 *Either Player A or Player B floats the volley toward Player C.*

Player C steps up to blitz the ball by hitting it on the fly, powering the ball into Player B's alley or to the middle, then continues to the net.

Player A squeezes the side on which the ball is hit.

Player D holds.

57 *Player C lobs to Player B's backhand side.*

Player B runs around the lob to hit an overhead.

Player A holds her position.

Player C holds her position.

Player D holds her position if the lob is deep, otherwise she retreats.

58 *Player C lobs to Player A's backhand side.*

Player A runs around the shot and hits an overhead.

Player B holds.

Player C stays back.

Player D holds or retreats, depending on lob quality.

59

Player C hits a high ground stroke to either Player A or Player B.

The hitter, either A or B, must take one step back and jump up, attempting to hit the ball. If the hitter makes contact, she has prolonged the point. If she misses, the point was lost anyway, because the ball was hit too low to run back and get it.

Player C holds her position.

Player D holds her position.

Fancy Switches

On occasion, all that you can do is run down the ball and hope to stay in the point. If your partner makes a great save on one shot, the responsibility to stay in the point often shifts to you. You must get the ball back, try to stabilize the situation, and untangle yourselves later.

KEYS TO FANCY SWITCHES
1. *Don't quit on your partner.*
2. *Stay in the point by proper movement.*

60 *Player C hits the ball to Player B.*

Player A holds the net.

Player B hits around Player D into the gap.

Player C runs down the ball and switches. Player C should hit the ball straight, deep to deep.

Player D stays in the point by crossing over to the side vacated by Player C. It is very important that Player D does not quit the point simply because the ball went past her.

Player A charges the net, since her partner was invited to go on the offensive.

61 *Player C hits the ball wide to Player A, pulling him off the court.*

Player B slides to the middle.

Player A makes his shot.

Player C's next shot is close to the singles line on Player A's side.

Player B goes for the ball. As Player A reenters the court, he crosses behind Player B.

62

Player C hits the ball crosscourt.

Player B tries to pick off the shot but misses. If Player B has not gone too far past the middle, he goes back to his original side. If Player B misses the shot but has moved too far over, he is stuck.

Player A must hit the shot deep to deep, then switch over.

Points in Progress—Both Back Plays

On occasion, it may be necessary for both you and your partner to stay back at the baseline. This may occur if your partner cannot hit crosscourt and the opposite net person is killing you. Or it may occur because the opposite net player is a great poacher and is killing you. Or it may occur because your net player is a weak volleyer and prefers not being at the net.

KEYS TO BOTH BACK
1. *Stay in the point.*
2. *Play offensively when invited in.*

63

Player C hits the ball in the middle between Players A and B.

Players A and B both go for the ball. One player calls for the ball; the other must yield to her partner and move out of the way.

If **Player C** stayed back, the return goes deep to Player C.

If **Player C** came in to the net, the hitter must escape.

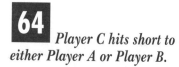

64 *Player C hits short to either Player A or Player B.*

Players A and B both run to hit the approach shot, then move in toward the net.

Player C stays in or back.

Player D holds her position.

$\mathscr{P}$LAYING *YOUR* BEST TENNIS

...
THE SEVEN
AREAS OF
SUPERIORITY

$\mathscr{I}$n my book *Essential Tennis*, I talked about the seven areas in which you, and now your partner, must be superior. These are *shot mechanics*, *play program*, *conditioning*, *attitude*, *state of mind*, *heart*, and *fortitude*. Recently, one of my teams came to me after losing a frustrating match. They thought that they should have won because they were so much better than their opponents. But when we reviewed the seven areas, they found that in fact, they were superior in only two of the seven areas. They were not the better team; they should have lost and did.

Shot Mechanics

All your confidence in your tennis game flows from your belief in your shots. If you know you have good form and good shot mechanics, you walk onto the court with confidence. The better your form, the more likely you are to hit good shots and continue to grow as a player. Good form intimidates opponents. The more you know and understand your art form, the easier it is for you to hold together and make the necessary corrections and adjustments during the match.

Play Program

This book is designed to teach you the doubles plays you need to know so that you and your partner will play in sync. Both you and your partner should be studying this book on a regular basis so that the proper drill scenario responses become automatic.

Conditioning

Your conditioning must be good enough to enable you to play both long points and long matches. Good conditioning means that you can expend energy from the first point to the very last one. At a recent U.S. Open tournament, one parent told his son to start slowly to conserve his energy. This advice worked; the young player started so slowly that he lost the first set! If you want to play serious tennis, you must condition your body to help you achieve your goal.

Attitude

You need to walk onto the court with a high level of self-respect and appreciation. You need to be arrogant. You need to believe that your team is deserving of the win and that you are ready to play. You need to have high energy and good body language throughout the match. As Stefan Edberg and Pete Sampras made their move into the number one spot, they worked hard on positive body language.

It is important that you stay arrogant. No one makes all the shots, but if you miss one or two and then start to mope and droop your shoulders, you are acting defeated. You must maintain your confidence; understand that you can withstand a few failures.

Step onto the court with a winner's attitude. Expect to win.

You must also step out onto the court with a level of respect for your partner. If you are upset that someone is your partner and believe that he or she can't hit a ball, that your partnership stands no chance of winning, then you won't! For a partnership to work, both players must be mutually supportive. If you continually question your partner's judgment, you not only intimidate but also demoralize him or her. During the match, you must be supportive if you want a chance to win.

State of Mind

Recently I was listening to Charlie Rose interview internationally acclaimed concert violinist Nadia Salerno-Sonenberg. When asked if she was ever intimidated by the hall in which she was about to play, she responded with an answer that is as appropriate to tennis as it is to music or any other situation that requires a positive focus. She stated that when she plays, she does not think about where she is playing or the quality of the orchestra or the concert hall, nor can she allow herself to be intimidated by those with whom she is playing. Whether she is to play for half an hour or two hours straight does not matter. When she plays she goes into a "zone of concentration" and blocks out all other thoughts but her playing. That's what I call a great state of mind!

State of mind means coming to the tennis court with a clear focus on the match at hand. You must be focused solely on tennis, not thinking about the four tasks you did before the match or need to do after the match. Do not be concerned with things beyond your control such as the sun, the wind, the temperature, the court, or the ball quality. Remember that both sides share the same disadvantages; that is the beauty of tennis. The frequent changeovers level the playing field, so stop fretting and stay focused.

Heart

I hope that you have already developed a love for the game. No one wins all the time, and some losses are tougher to handle than others. But it is the love of the game that allows you to endure a loss and rebound with an even stronger will to win. Many days, mastering all seven areas of superiority is difficult to do, but the love of the game should sustain you. There is not one high-level player alive who at some point in his or her career did not want to quit the game after experiencing moments of frustration. But it is the ability to work hard both on and off the court that creates success. And that work requires a lot of heart.

Fortitude

You must develop the fortitude to do what is necessary on and off the court. Often my players will come to me complaining of a loss. Although they can articulate what had to be done to win the match, they did not have the fortitude to execute those requirements. It takes courage to continue to fight; recognize the task to be accomplished, then divide it into achievable goals and do it.

...
BECOMING A BETTER TEAM

*I*n a good team, each player helps the other out. It stands to reason that the more you play with the same partner, the more you will develop a sense of how to help each other. Practicing the drills in this book enhances the partnership. It also helps to know how each of you will respond to the different scenarios you may encounter on the court. Study this book to reaffirm what is to be done in each situation. You and your partner may even be able to work out some variations on these drills to make you a more effective team.

Signaling

Once you reach the 3.0 level, to function better as a team you must implement a signal system, because your opponents will be good enough to consistently aim the ball to avoid the net player. If the net player is not an active participant, the back player will be trying to hold serve but playing at a disadvantage, two against one. The use of signals enhances your offense and intimidates your opponents.

At all levels of play, the net player must help his or her partner hold serve. Often the stronger player loses serve but the weaker player holds. This anomaly occurs because the stronger player receives little help from the net player. When the weaker player serves, the stronger player often wins two points at the net, thus making a service hold easier.

THE PLAY OPTIONS

On the serve, there are three possible determinants for movement. The net player may move spontaneously, causing the server to read his or her partner and adjust accordingly. I do not encourage this system because it gives the server one more job to do. Besides having to follow the opponent's shot, the server must also be looking at his or her partner for possible movement—a distraction at best.

The second scenario occurs during a brief get-together between the players, called a huddle, where a play is decided on for both the first and second serves. Although this is a good strategy, the catch is that the players must remember both plays.

The third system requires the use of hand signals on each serve—the preferred system. Since a play is agreed on by the partners moments before each serve, there is little chance for error or forgetting the play. Each serve can have a new play, with the server verbally acknowledging the net player's selection. Of course, the server always has the option of overruling the net player's call.

THE THREE SIGNALS

The open hand indicates that the net person will poach. After serving the ball, the server must initially step into the court on his or her side to put on a fake; otherwise, the server tips the play. If the server is going to the net, he or she moves in two steps straight ahead before

Poach signal

breaking off on the diagonal to quickly change sides. If the server is staying back, after the serve is hit, he or she holds the spot for one count, then quickly changes sides.

The two fingers down sign indicates that the net player is going to fake poaching. This play is very important because, when the net player moves, the serve returner does not know where the net player will go. On this play, the net player takes two hard steps on the run as if to poach, then quickly returns to the original spot. The server either goes straight to the net or stays back on the original side.

The *closed hand* indicates that the net person is staying; there is no poach. On this play, the server either moves in to the net or stays behind the baseline on the original side.

WHERE DO YOU AIM THE SERVE?

Some teams like to signal the server where to place the serve. Thumb up means serve to the right; index finger out means serve to the left. I find that the call of serve placement becomes redundant, because the play itself dictates serve placement.

Fake poach signal   *Staying signal*

Serve to the right signal

Serve to the left signal

Many players serve up the middle in doubles all the time. When you are running the poach play, it is very important that the serve be placed up the middle because it closes off the easy down-the-line shot, the counter to the poach. On the other two plays, fake and stay, the serve can be aimed anywhere. When you play the I formation or Australian, the predominant serve location is up the middle.

WHERE DO YOU AIM THE SERVE RETURN?

Generally, the returner should hit the return away from the stationary net player. Thus, most doubles returns go crosscourt. If the serve side is lined up in the Australian formation, then follow the principle of going away from the stationary net player and return down the line.

Before the serve is struck, the returner must decide where to place the return, then execute that decision, trusting that he or she will do a better job than the net player. As long as you keep looking up to ensure that you are hitting the ball to the open zone, you will miss because you are not focusing on the ball. Forget the opposition; just hit the ball.

Holding the Game Together

There are three things that must be done to keep your game in tact: *watch the ball*, *stay focused*, and maintain a *discipline of execution*.

WATCH THE BALL

Although watching the ball seems easy, it is not. Just the fact that there is another body on your side of the net often creates a visual distraction. In the course of play, it is easy to become caught up in looking where you want to hit the ball instead of watching the ball. That's why this book and these plays are so crucial—they teach you where the ball should go, so you need never look up. Although you must know where to hit the ball, you do not scout out the area then recheck to make sure it is right. Many mistakes occur because the hitter is looking where the ball is going instead of ensuring proper execution before admiring his or her handiwork.

Don't be a "nice guy." I often hear my students say, "I was going to hit it in the right area, close to close, but I saw Joan in the way so I looked at her instead of the ball." The opposing net player must understand that the ball may come at or near him or her and should be prepared for it.

Your job is to hit the ball in the proper area; the opponent's is to defend his or her area. Your job as the hitter is to watch the ball and execute. The opponent's job is to try to stop you. When I play doubles, I usually get hit once or twice in a match when standing at the net. I am not mad at my opponent when this happens; in fact, I like the ball coming at me. At point-blank net play, there is so little reaction time that if you go right at me I am able to reflex the ball back into the court four out of five times.

But on the point-blank shots that go around me, I make only one in five, since there is no time for any movement. I will gladly take the occasional hit at my body to get more balls back, because I can take care of myself. It greatly helps my team when the opponent is fearful of being too aggressive, worried about hitting me. When your play level is so superior to that of the others on the court that you could consistently hit anywhere on the court, work on put-away angles when at the net.

WHEN DO YOU WATCH THE BALL?

When your partner is serving—after you have made sure that your partner is ready to serve—you look forward because you know where the ball is going to go. Unless it goes into the service square, there will be no point to play. At all other times, follow the ball. Some pros like to look straight ahead to read their opponents' reaction. Others like to know where the ball is at all times. By following the ball as soon as your partner strikes the shot, you know where it is going, which helps you prepare for the next shot. It also helps your concentration, because you are always focused on the ball. Follow the ball by glimpsing back over your shoulder, but try not to imitate a rotisserie chicken.

STAY FOCUSED

During a match, very little court time is spent actually hitting the ball, so it is critical that you learn how to stay focused between points and between games. The huddle system will keep you focused. Never get involved with your opponents. How they look, hit, or act is their problem; don't make it yours. Occasionally, my students will comment that their opponents' shots or form was so strange that they were distracted and could not hit. Or they didn't like the way the opponents treated them. You must learn how to stay focused on your side of the net, in a positive fashion.

You must trust and use your mechanics and play program. Initially, as you are learning the different plays and responses, you must do a lot of thinking. Your goal, however, is to automate the appropriate response; through repetition, you will run the correct plays. Remember, you must concentrate on the task at hand. Hit the ball with your learned form, and be willing to work the point.

There are five levels of focus delivery: long-point play ability, next point, next game, next set, next day. It is common after a long point to take a mental rest and self-cancel because you are exhausted from that previous point. You wind up not playing the current or next point. Television commentators call these "loose points." Loose points lead to loose games. Loose games lead to loose sets. Loose sets lead to lots of losses.

START RITUALS

To facilitate concentration, you must have start rituals.

SERVER'S START RITUAL

1. *Determine the strategy play with your partner.*

2. *Decide to serve and volley or stay back.*

3. *Decide where to place the serve.*

4. *Bounce the ball one to four times.*

5. *Breathe.*

6. *Hit the ball.*

SERVER'S PARTNER'S RITUAL

1. Signal the strategy play to the server.

2. Lightly bounce on your toes to get ready to play the upcoming point.

SERVE RETURNER'S RITUAL

1. Lightly bounce on your toes to prepare to play the upcoming point.

2. Review your targets—crosscourt or down the line.

3. Decide to go forward or stay back.

4. Bounce on your toes as the server begins the motion.

5. Take one step forward as the toss goes up.

6. As the ball is struck, take a second step with both feet—a split step forward.

7. Read and react to the serve and stay committed to your form.

SERVE RETURNER'S PARTNER'S RITUAL

1. Lightly bounce on your toes to be ready for the upcoming point.

HUDDLING IN BETWEEN POINTS

❶ Keep the focus on your side. Don't get caught up in what the other team is doing.

❷ Quickly get together. You are allowed 20 seconds between points. Say, "Great shot, Sallie" or "Oops, sorry partner."

❸ Reconfirm the positive and get back to the game plan. "Let's go. We'll get this one."

❹ If you missed, take a swing at the shot the correct way. Remind your muscles of the proper stroke.

Huddling in between points

REGROUPING

When you are missing your shots, you must remain focused and positive. If you make your partner spend energy pumping you up, your partner will have no energy left for his or her own game. Although it is both players' responsibility to help the other on occasion, you cannot make it a full-time job. The key to remember is that *the form never fails you; you fail the form*. The easiest way to correct mistakes is to take a practice swing after a miss, going over the shot in your head with the correct video of that shot running. To help you deal more specifically with your mistakes, here is a quick checklist:

➤ When you are missing, forget the huddle for one second.

➤ Take a practice swing, recreating the shot properly.

➤ Close your eyes and run the video in your head of the shot as it is supposed to be performed. Never buy the idea that this is a day when your shots don't work. Remember: The form never fails you; you fail the form.

Regrouping in between games

As you change sides, you must stay focused on this match only.

- *Relax, towel off, drink, and stay cool for a few seconds.*

- *Review the game plan for the next game with your partner.*

- *Remind each other of where the sun is and from which direction the wind is blowing.*

- *Review the weaknesses you have discovered and pledge to attack them.*

MAINTAIN A DISCIPLINE OF EXECUTION

Players often complain to me that even though they were watching the ball and focused on the match, they still missed. Why? You must have the ability to discipline yourself to implement your knowledge and execute your form on every hit. Recently on ESPN, the commentators were analyzing Troy Aikman, the quarterback for the Dallas Cowboys, and another quarterback. The comparison showed the same play being run: Aikman ran the play with executed discipline, but the other quarterback did not. Even when you know what to do, you must still make yourself perform.

The ability to perform consistently takes work, practice, and patience. Part of being a winner is being willing to work on the shots. Until you can perform your shots competently every day, when each one automatically flows off your racquet—a level many of the top pros never reach—you must talk to yourself in a positive manner and work your way through the shot. Discipline yourself to play at your skill level and knowledge level each time you play.

CHAPTER 7.

CORRECTING MISTAKES

.....................*O*ccasionally you'll find yourself frustrated by your performance on the court, when you're seemingly unable to hit a shot of one kind or another that will go over the net and stay inside the court boundaries. Here is a quick checklist for those troublesome times. Often if you observe how you are missing, you will be able to figure out why you are missing and then be able to correct your mistakes.

GROUND STROKES

➤ *PROBLEM: You are hitting into the net.*

SOLUTION: You are making contact too late, thus you don't generate enough body power. Prepare earlier.

SOLUTION: Your wrist may be rolling over or caving in. Hit the ball dead center so the impact of the hit does not turn your racquet so forcefully.

SOLUTION: You may have mishit the ball. Watch the ball better; keep your head down and still longer.

SOLUTION: If the stroke feels good and looks good but still lands in the net, then your alignment was over the ball, without enough low-to-high contact. To correct, bend down more.

SOLUTION: If the stroke feels awful and the ball went nowhere, your body moved but your arm and racquet did not. Make sure that you act and move as a unit: upper body, lower body, arm, and racquet all moving together at the same time.

➤ PROBLEM: *You are hitting the ball wide.*

SOLUTION: Your balance may be pulled too much toward the aimed direction; balance better.

SOLUTION: You may have aimed too wide. Don't go for the lines; instead, aim for a target area that allows for a greater margin of error.

➤ PROBLEM: *You are hitting the ball long.*

SOLUTION: You may be hitting slightly late. When there is not enough spin placed on the hit, it misses some gravitational resistance. To correct, attack the ball; don't let the ball play you.

SOLUTION: If the ball floats long, your racquet head probably dropped below the wrist, so always keep the racquet head up. This is straight geometry: If your racquet creates an up angle, the ball will go up.

SOLUTION: If you powered the ball long, either you slapped at the ball with your wrist—an excellent hockey form, but a lousy tennis form—or your arm and racquet exploded. To correct slapping, swing with your arm and racquet together as a unit. To correct exploding, remind yourself that tennis is a boundary sport, so you must learn to harness your energy. If the arm and racquet wildly win a race with the rest of your body, the shot will sail, so remember the unit movement concept.

R E T U R N I N G
S E R V E

➤ PROBLEM: *You are having difficulty returning serve.*

SOLUTION: The corrections for serve return are the same as those for ground strokes. In addition, if you are having difficulty returning serve, have the net person come back to the baseline so there is no power target for the opponents. The returner should aim up the middle of the court to keep the ball in play. As the returner's confidence grows, he or she may feel more at ease trying to return away from the net player, so his or her partner can return to the offensive net position.

··· VOLLEYS

➤ *PROBLEM:* **You are missing your volleys long.**

SOLUTION: You may be taking too much of a backswing, which is the most common volley mistake. Too much backswing results in a late and wild hit, which sends the ball all over the court. To correct, make sure that your racquet starts in front of you. Try to keep the racquet head within your sight; if the racquet is behind you, this will be impossible.

SOLUTION: You may be running through the volley. When your opponent hits the ball, it is critical that you do a split step or neutral step that puts your body on balance so you will be able to move in the direction of the incoming ball.

SOLUTION: Don't drop your wrist. Make sure that your racquet head stays above your wrist. If the racquet drops, the racquet angle makes the ball go up.

➤ *PROBLEM:* **You are hitting your volleys in the net.**

SOLUTION: If you are missing because you are mishitting, track the ball better. Don't look where the ball is going—don't even peek at the destination.

SOLUTION: Your wrist caves in, so the ball goes nowhere. Brace better for the impact.

➤ *PROBLEM:* **You are hitting your volleys wide.**

SOLUTION: Don't go for so much precision.

SOLUTION: Make sure that your racquet is not angled so severely that it is impossible for the ball to land in the court.

··· SERVING

➤ *PROBLEM:* **Your service toss is all over the sky.**

SOLUTION: You are not giving yourself a chance at success. This is where new players often get stuck. If every toss varies greatly, so will every hit motion in reaction to the varied tosses. Since every toss is an adventure in space, there is no growth pattern. To correct, slow down, making sure that the tossing arm is relaxed. Then work on the five elements of the toss. The second point to remember is to make sure that your toss is being released as you are going forward.

FIVE TOSS ELEMENTS

1. *Same downswing spot.*

2. *Same upswing spot.*

3. *Same rhythm of swing of the arm.*

4. *Have the toss release come only out the "top door"—no "side" exits.*

5. *Whenever the toss arm comes down, let it softly collapse onto your body.*

SOLUTION: To help target your toss, toss the ball into a basketball hoop or into a post at the side of the court. For some players, the toss clock is too vague. By using a real target, a beginning player can visualize the toss-control concept.

➤ PROBLEM: *Your service hit misses into the net.*

SOLUTION: You have hit down on the ball; the geometric angle created has no chance of clearing the net. If your toss was not high enough in the first place—reaching only as high as your nose—you will find it difficult to hit up. Swing the toss arm more to get more toss height.

SOLUTION: Your toss hand and head came down too soon. Keep your tossing arm and head up longer. Many players are so worried about hitting their tossing arm that they yank it away quickly, which pulls their shoulders and weight down. Try to sight the toss through your tossing hand, which forces you to stay tall on the serve.

SOLUTION: If your toss was good initially but the ball was too low by the time you hit it, you did not go up to the ball. This is a tough one for new players. What allows you to chase the ball with a constant attack speed is the belief that the toss is going to be in the same reasonable location every time.

SOLUTION: If the toss is always radically different, it is nearly impossible to spot and find an errant toss. To correct, trust your toss and stay aggressive. If you serve in segments, the power goes away; go up after the ball.

SOLUTION: Did you bend your knees enough? For those of you who have added the knee bend, this is a big part of your motion that helps you get under the ball. Learn to relax and not rush your motion; you must incorporate this integral part each time.

➤ PROBLEM: *Your service hit is long.*

SOLUTION: The toss is behind you. You are hitting the ball too early in the motion, getting only the hitting up part, so toss the ball more in front of you.

SOLUTION: Did you push it long? If the toss is too low, you will get under it too much and just push it up, so toss the ball higher.

SOLUTION: Your feet may have moved too much. If you go for a walk and get no wrist action because the toss is too far right or left, you will come out of the over-your-head motion and push the ball out. Bring the toss back into the target range.

➤ PROBLEM: *Your service hit is wide.*

SOLUTION: Remember that when you serve you must drive your motion into the target box. Don't aim too finely; don't go for the lines. Give yourself a wider target area. Inexperienced players especially should aim for the middle of the square on the second serve to prevent double-faulting.

• • •
OVERHEADS

➤ PROBLEM: *Your overhead lands in the net.*

SOLUTION: The ball dropped too low. When the ball drops too low, it is difficult not to overhit it down, resulting in no clearance. To correct, prepare earlier and reach up more.

SOLUTION: If you are mishitting, hitting the edge of your racquet, the ball will go nowhere. Keep your head up and watch the ball longer.

SOLUTION: If you hit the ball solidly on the overhead, you may be close enough to the net to hit the ball down and still have it clear the net. From close in this is easy, but as you step farther back, the angle changes and it becomes tougher, so hit the overhead more like your serve and spin it to a corner.

➤ PROBLEM: *Your overhead lands long.*

SOLUTION: You had no wrist action; you just pushed the ball up. As with the serve, you need to impart wrist action, so hit the overhead like a serve to spin the ball.

SOLUTION: If the ball sails long, you are probably hitting the ball late. Move your feet more and get behind the ball more so you can step up into the shot.

SOLUTION: You may have misjudged the flight pattern of the incoming lob, which is a universal problem. Step back more than you think you need to, then step up into the shot.

...
LOBS

> PROBLEM: *Your lob lands short or into the net.*

SOLUTION: Make sure that you give it a little more hit power. A lob is a measurement shot: Too little power will get you killed; too much causes you to miss. You need to develop soft hands to be able to feel and measure the stroke, which must be hit in front of you, dead center, and with enough ball-racquet contact time.

> PROBLEM: *Your lob lands long.*

SOLUTION: You may be feeling too much pressure from the net player, trying to make this shot too good. Again, you must develop the touch to measure this shot.

AFTERWORD

One of the most rewarding elements of my first book, *Essential Tennis*, is having readers repeatedly tell me how they refer to the book over and over again to study the concepts presented. That is my hope for the readers of *Winning Doubles*. I have presented a tremendous amount of information to help you become a better doubles player. The concepts are ones that will last forever and should be reviewed periodically to reinforce the knowledge you have gained. As you master the information, your confidence will grow, and as your confidence grows, your tennis will become more consistent. When the pros are asked what their greatest frustration is, they often say that two days ago they played great, but today their performance level has tapered off. Every player has a range of achievement, but this range must be kept small. You must perform at 85% or more of your skill and knowledge level every time you play on the court; as you master the material, you will.

In the playbook section, I showed you the right shot to hit, where to hit the ball, and where to reposition yourself to win your points more easily and effectively. When you play, you should never feel that you have to gamble or hit great shots to win. Steffi Graf's coach Heinz Gunthardt recently said that he was working with her to find the easiest way to win the point and help her recognize that when she is playing well, she hardly ever has to hit a great shot. This applies to all tennis players. Remember that tennis is a game of percentages; no one shot or strategy pays off every time. You may play the greatest point in the world, only to have your opponent steal it away from you with a lucky shot or mishit. That happens, but if you stay with the program I have designed for you, the percentages are weighted in your favor.

Your growth goal as you become a better team is to add more offense to your game plan. In doubles, offense is played at the net. As I explained earlier, the key is to learn your target area so that you or your partner can do damage with the volley and get a good percentage of payoff points. I constantly remind my students that by working on their games year in and year out, their games will continue to improve and evolve. Each match you will have a few more opportunities to convert playing points into winning opportunities, which is important for your team's mental well-being.

As you reach a higher level of play, your team may be pressed by opponents who reach the net before your team does. The really good players stay calm, acting like the opposing team is just bluffing its position, and hit an escape shot. Make one clear shot selection; do not change your mind and try to outexecute your opponents.

The section of the book on helping your partner is critical if you are to grow as a team. As a reminder, play well yourself, run the plays, employ a doubles attitude, and trust your partner. Learn how to talk to each other. Don't try to coach your partner, don't quit on your partner, and make sure that your equipment is technologically correct. The section on keeping the team in sync is critical for team growth. Make sure that your team has a game plan and that both your and your partner's computers are on so that your team can analyze the match conditions and components. Finally, learn to huddle, and have a good time with each other.

As Richey Renenberg said in the foreword, learn to love the interaction with your partner. As I mentioned in the beginning of the book, I have never had so much fun on the court as I have when playing with my current partner, Mark Jee. As a team, digest the materials presented, and let the wins start to roll your way.

USTA LEVELS OF THE GAME

To provide a better understanding of the levels of the game, the United States Tennis Association (USTA) has devised the following rating system:

1.0 This player is just starting to play tennis.

1.5 This player has limited experience and is still working primarily on getting the ball in play.

2.0 This player needs on-court experience. This player has obvious stroke weaknesses but is familiar with basic positions for singles and doubles play.

2.5 This player is learning to judge where the ball is going, although court coverage is weak. This player can sustain a slow-paced rally with other players of the same ability.

3.0 This player is consistent when hitting medium-paced shots but is not comfortable with all strokes and lacks control when trying for directional intent, depth, or power.

3.5 This player has achieved improved stroke dependability and direction on moderate shots but still lacks depth and variety. This player is starting to exhibit more aggressive net play, has improved court coverage, and is developing teamwork in doubles.

4.0 This player has dependable strokes, including directional intent and depth on both forehand and backhand sides on moderate shots, plus the ability to use lobs, overheads, approach shots, and volleys with some success. This player occasionally forces errors when serving, and teamwork in doubles is evident.

4.5 This player has begun to master the use of power and spins and is beginning to handle pace, has sound footwork, can control depth of shots, and is beginning to vary tactics according to opponents. This player can hit first serves with power and accuracy, can place the second serve, and is able to rush the net successfully.

5.0 This player has good shot anticipation and frequently has an outstanding shot or exceptional consistency around which a game can be structured. This player can regularly hit winners or force errors off short balls; can put away volleys; can successfully execute lobs, drop shots, half volleys, and overhead smashes; and has good depth and spin on most second serves.

5.5 This player has developed power or consistency or both as a major weapon. This player can vary strategies and styles of play in a competitive situation and hits dependable shots in stress situations.

6.0 These players generally do not need the USTA rating system. Ranking or past rankings will speak for themselves. The 6.0 player typically has had intensive training for 7.0 national tournament competition at the junior and collegiate levels and has obtained a sectional or national ranking or both.

6.5 This player has a reasonable chance of succeeding at the 7.0 level and has extensive satellite tournament experience.

7.0 This is a world-class player who is committed to tournament competition on the international level and whose major source of income is tournament prize winnings.

...
SCORING

In both singles and doubles, tennis matches are played in *sets*. To win a set, one player must win at least six games by a margin of two. Thus the score can be 6–0 through 6–4 but not 6–5, which would require one more game to be played. If the score becomes 7–5, the set is over, but if the opponent ties it at 6–6, a *tiebreaker* is played (more on this in a moment).

Most matches consist of a two-out-of-three-set format, except for the Grand Slam, Davis Cup, and a few other pro tournaments, where the men play three-out-of-five-set matches. The only women's event to use the three-out-of-five-set format is the culmination tournament of the tour finals.

There are two ways to score a *game* of tennis: *no ad* and *regular* scoring. In the no ad (short for no advantage) format, the first player to win four points wins the game. Thus when the score is 3–3, only one more point is played, and the opponent has the preference as to which side the server must serve. Many tournaments use this scoring method to move the sets along. No ad is also a good scoring method when court time is limited.

In the regular scoring method, one player must still win four points, but by a margin of two. Zero points is called love; one point is called 15; two points, 30; three points, 40. After 40–40, called *deuce*, there are no more numbers. At deuce, both players are two points away from winning the game. If the server wins the deuce point, that player needs just one more point to win, which is his or her advantage, called "ad in." If the server wins the next point, he or she has won the game. But if the opponent wins the deuce point, it's "ad out." If the receiver loses the next point, the score is tied again at deuce. Whoever scores next will have the advantage, which continues until one player wins the deuce and following point.

Points are scored by hitting a winning shot or the opponent missing a shot.

The serving square in which the deuce point can be played is often referred to as the deuce court. The serving square in which the ad point is played is called the ad court.

Holding serve means that the server has won the game; the serve was held. *Breaking serve* means that the opponent has won the server's game.

Some players use slang terminology in scoring. Fifteen, the first point, is sometimes shortened to 5. "Deuce" might be said at 30 all, since both players need two points to win. When recounting set scores, there is no need to mention the first number (6), since it is a given, so the player says that he or she won in three and five, meaning 6–3, 7–5.

189

...
USTA CODE OF CONDUCT

To ensure the highest type of sportsmanship, the United States Tennis Association (USTA) has established a code of conduct that every player is expected to follow. Excerpts from the official USTA publication "The Code," whose principles and guidelines apply in any match conducted without officials, are as follows:

- If you have any doubt as to whether a ball is out or good, you must give your opponent the benefit of the doubt and play the ball as good. You should *not* play a let.

- It is your obligation to call all balls on your side, to help your opponent make calls when the opponent requests it, and to *call against yourself* (with the exception of the first service) any ball that you clearly see out on your opponent's side of the net.

- Any "out" or "let" call must be made *instantaneously* (i.e., made before either an opponent has hit the return or the return has gone out of play); otherwise, the ball continues in play.

- Do *not* enlist the aid of spectators in making line calls.

- If you call a ball out and then realize it was good, you should correct your call.

- To avoid controversy over the score, the server should announce the set score (e.g., 5–4) before starting a game and the game score (e.g., 30–40) prior to serving each point.

- If players cannot agree on the score, they may go back to the last score on which there was agreement and resume play from that point, or they may spin a racquet.

- Foot faults are not allowed. If an opponent persists in foot-faulting after being warned not to do so, the referee should be informed.

- Wait until the players on another court have completed a point before retrieving or returning a ball.

- Once you have entered a tournament, honor your commitment to play. Exceptions should occur only in cases of serious illness, injury, or personal emergency.

- From the beginning of the match, play must be continuous. Attempts to stall or extend rest periods for the purpose of recovering from a loss of physical condition (such as cramps or shortness of breath) are clearly illegal.

- Intentional distractions that interfere with your opponent's concentration or effort to play the ball are against the rules.

- Spectators, including parents, friends, and coaches, are welcome to watch and enjoy matches. Their role, however, is clearly restricted to that of passive observer, with *no involvement of any kind* during the match.

- Players are expected to put forth a full and honest effort regardless of the score or expected outcome.

- Players are expected to maintain full control over their emotions and the resulting behavior throughout the match. If you begin to lose your composure during play, try the following: Take several deep breaths. Exhale as slowly as possible and feel your muscles relax. Concentrate on your own game and behavior while ignoring distractions from your opponent or surroundings.

- Be your own best friend—enjoy your good shots and forget the poor ones.

At the competitive level, there is a three-pronged penalty system for violating the rules of behavior. The first violation incurs a warning, the second costs a point, and the third results in a defaulted match. Although the pros do a certain amount of arguing with the officials, technically, arguing is not allowed, and it sets a poor example.